SOME IMPRESSIONS

OF THE

UNITED STATES

SOME IMPRESSIONS

OF THE

UNITED STATES

BY

EDWARD A. FREEMAN

BOOKS FOR LIBRARIES PRESS
FREEPORT, NEW YORK

First Published 1883
Reprinted 1970

STANDARD BOOK NUMBER:
8369-5328-2

LIBRARY OF CONGRESS CATALOG CARD NUMBER:
76-117875

PRINTED IN THE UNITED STATES OF AMERICA

PREFACE.

THIS small book is founded on four articles
which have appeared in the "Fortnightly Review" for August and September 1882 and in
"Longman's Magazine" for November 1882 and
January 1883. The substance of those articles is
here, together with an amount of new matter
at least as large as the articles themselves. They
represent observations made in the United States
during a stay which lasted from October 1881
to April 1882. In the course of that stay I
saw something of most of the chief Northern
States; but I did not get further west than
St. Louis, or further south than the northern
part of Virginia. The "impressions" are of course
those of one who looks at things for his own
purposes and from his own point of view. I
have, I hope, never forgotten that there are many

other points of view from which the same things
may be looked at. But I believe that each man
does best by keeping to his own line, and not
meddling with inquiries foreign to that line and
in which he would most likely go wrong.

SOMERLEAZE, WELLS:
February 16, 1883.

CONTENTS.

CONTENTS. vii

SOME IMPRESSIONS

OF THE

UNITED STATES.

SOME IMPRESSIONS

OF

THE UNITED STATES.

I.

I HAVE been asked to say something as to the
impressions left on my mind by my late visit to
the United States. This is a work which I should
hardly have undertaken of my own choice. But
it seemed to be gradually laid upon me by force
of circumstances. He who visits Britain from
America, he who visits America from Britain,
seems bound, if he be at all in the habit of using
the pen, to use it forthwith to set down all or some
of his impressions of the kindred land and its people. The thing seems to have taken its place as
a formal duty which cannot be escaped. For my
own part I had hoped to escape it. I was so well
treated in America that it really seemed unthank-
ful, almost uncivil, for me to write anything about
America. Yet, while I was there, I was asked

over and over again, whether I meant to write a
book about America. All thought of writing a
book I could then honestly disclaim. It was only
gradually that the necessity even of writing something less than a book forced itself upon me. The
thought of a book I still disclaimed long after I
had found myself in print on the subject. But as
the detached papers were laid upon me by circumstances, so at a later stage the graver duty was laid
upon me. And I, who wished at first to escape
from making even an article, now find myself making a book.

I still regret the necessity; for I feel that any
picture that I can draw of American things must
necessarily be an imperfect one, much more imperfect than the picture which I might draw of
any European land. For there are many aspects
of any country, but above all of a young country,
of which I am quite unfit to judge, and at which
indeed I was not likely to look at all. And this
necessary imperfection is a worse fault in a young
country than it is in an old one. In a young country everything is affected by the fact of youth, in
a way in which things in an old country are not
always affected by the fact of age. It is always
better, if possible, to make present and past illustrate one another; still in an old country it is often

easy, from some points of view, to treat of the present with very little reference to the past, and of the past with very little reference to the present. But in a young country the nearness of even the remotest past has a direct influence on the present. Everything seems to be young together, while in an old country some things are old and some young. This air of newness in the United States is often, as I hope presently to show, only an air; but the air of seeming newness practically affects everything. It seems to bring different classes of things more nearly to a level than they are in an old country. It is not so easy as it is in an old country to keep things apart from each other. And unluckily there are a great many aspects of present life, aspects which are specially prominent in American life, which for me have no interest whatever. Political and judicial assemblies have for me the same interest in young America which they have in old Greece. But, greatly to my ill-luck, I am wholly ignorant of all things bearing on commerce, manufactures, or agriculture. Nor am I better skilled in matters bearing on education, unless it be education which rises to the level of a college or university. Now I can pass through an old country, say Italy or Dalmatia, and I can find a great deal to notice and to record without meddling with any of the things of which I am ignorant. In America it is hardly possible to avoid them. Happily my American friends were merciful. I was taken to see a good many schools; for some people, I know not why, seemed to think that I had something to do with schools, or at least that I took some special interest in schools. But I was spared the more fearful grind of going through factories, prisons, hospitals, with all the weariness of an inexpert.

It follows therefore at once that any remarks of mine on American matters must be very imperfect, and further that such imperfection is a much greater fault in the case of America than it might be in the case of some other lands. But beyond this, I take up my pen with a dread that anything that I can say of the United States and their people will be frightfully one-sided. It is not easy to write quite impartially of a land in which a man has received so cordial a welcome and such constant and unmixed kindness as I received in America. One has a feeling that it is ungrateful, almost unfair, to write anything but unmixed praise; and yet unmixed praise, either in America or anywhere else, must be unfair, because it must be untruthful. And I feel too that I personally can have seen only some of the brightest sides of the country and its people. The whole nation cannot be as good as the people who have been so good to me. I was naturally thrown mainly among men whose thoughts and pursuits had some kind of likeness to my own. I lived chiefly with professors, lawyers, a sprinkling of statesmen, men of thought and information of various kinds. Of the pushing, meddling, questioning American, described in so many stories and caricatures, I have seen nothing, at least not on American soil. It is therefore somewhat hard for me to write about American matters at all. But I think that cultivated and sensible people in America, such as those among whom I spent most of my time when I was there, are not likely to be offended with anything that I am likely to say. I trust at least that they will not be displeased with a certain general doctrine which I have to maintain, and at which I have already hinted. This is that the seeming newness of everything in the United States is very superficial, and that there is a large kernel of what is old within. If a formula is wanted, I would put it in this shape. There are many things in the United States which are new, very new, palpably new at first sight. But when a thing is not thus palpably new it is commonly quite as old as the thing that answers to it in England, and very often much older.

II.

"What do you think of our country?" is the question traditionally put into the mouth of the American addressing his British visitor. And the British visitor in real life finds that he very often has to answer that question or its equivalent. In its naked shape it is not often put by the very best people, and, whenever it is put by any one, the question is a little embarrassing. It is not a question that one can answer offhand in words of one syllable. I have sometimes tried to turn it off by answering that their country was very big, a statement which is surely colourless and which cannot be denied by people of any way of thinking. Or I have tried to parry it by asking whether they meant the whole Union or their own particular State or neighbourhood. But even when one is not questioned quite so nakedly, it is easy to see an intense desire on the part of the American host to know how everything about him looks in the eyes of the British guest. Such a desire is indeed almost inherent in the relation of host and guest everywhere; but it seems to be stronger than elsewhere, it certainly is more openly and pressingly revealed than elsewhere, when the host is American and the guest British. That so it

should be is neither wonderful nor blameable. It
is only in the nature of things that every American
should, in his heart, deem British opinion more
important than any other, and should in his heart
value British good opinion more fondly than any
other. A young nation, honestly conscious of its
own greatness in many ways, but conscious at the
same time that it has been often unfairly censured,
often misunderstood, is sure to be keenly sensitive
to the opinion of other nations, and above all of
the nation which in its heart it feels to be its own
parent. The very tone of boasting and bluster
towards Europe and England which is sometimes
put on by some classes of American writers and
speakers is really a witness to this feeling. American dislike towards England—when it is really
felt and not put on simply to catch Irish votes—
is something quite different from certain forms of
national ill-feeling to which we are used at home.
It is unlike either the old-fashioned dislike to
France or the new-fashioned dislike to Russia.
In this last kind of dislike there is mingled a certain feeling of contempt, of very unjust contempt
in both cases, but still of genuine contempt. It is
the dislike which springs from old-standing national
self-sufficiency, a dislike which is quite free from
touchiness or inquisitiveness ; no British character-

istic is more marked than our utter and often most foolish heedlessness of the opinion of other nations. This is the natural weakness of an old nation, above all of an insular nation. The natural weakness of a young nation is the exact opposite. Such a nation must be conscious; it must be touchy; it must be inquisitive. It cannot help caring for the opinion of other nations, above all for the opinion of its own ancient mother-land. And if such a nation, truly or untruly, fancies itself slighted, misrepresented, misunderstood, if it fails to meet with sympathy where it seeks for sympathy, the result may easily be a dislike which is possibly real, a contempt which is certainly artificial. This innate yearning, often unavowed, sometimes perhaps unconscious, for European, above all for British, good opinion often shows itself in odd ways. One form of it is the tendency in some Americans, chiefly perhaps in some American newspapers—a tendency which to us seems so strange—to conjure up slights where nothing like a slight has been meant. This form of interest is unpleasant, but it is not at all unnatural. The honest desire to know what the stranger, above all what the British stranger, thinks is another and a better side of the same feeling. It may sometimes get a little ludicrous and a little wearisome; but in moderation it is perfectly right

and healthy. And with the highest class of Americans—those who do not put their questions in quite
so naked a shape, those who are keen-sighted enough
to understand and candid enough to avow that there
may be a balance of merit and defect either way—
the discussion of things on the older and the newer
side of Ocean often leads to comparisons, and the
comparisons often lead to investigations, which
are interesting and instructive in the highest
degree.

Now comparisons and investigations of this kind
come most naturally when there is a strong essential
likeness between the things compared. It is in
such cases, not in those where the things compared
are altogether unlike one another, that we note the
minutest differences. It is where things are very
much alike that we most diligently mark the points
in which they are not alike. Take for instance the
two universities of Oxford and Cambridge. The
main features in the constitution and customs of
the two are so closely alike to one another, and so
utterly unlike those of any other universities in the
world, that there is a certain curious pleasure in
tracing out the endless minute points in which they
differ. So it is between England and America. It
is the essential likeness which makes us note every
point of unlikeness. I hardly know whether my

American friends were pleased or disappointed—
they certainly were sometimes a little surprised—
at my telling them, as I often had to do, that what
most struck me in their country was how little it
differed from my own. I had to say over and over
again that this was the thing which had most surprised me, but that on second thoughts it did not
surprise me at all, as it was only what was perfectly
natural. To me most certainly the United States
did not seem a foreign country; it was simply
England with a difference. The difference struck
me as certainly greater than the greatest difference
which had ever struck me between one part of
England and another, but as certainly less than the
difference which strikes me when I enter Scotland.
That America should seem less strange than Scotland is doubtless partly owing to the fact that English and Scottish law are two things which stand
wholly apart, while the law of the American States
is for the most part simply English law with a
difference. All things therefore which depend on
the administration of the law—and the things which
depend on the administration of the law make up a
good part of ordinary life—are different between
England and Scotland, while they are largely the
same between England and America. A crowd of
names, offices, formulæ, modes of proceeding, are

very much the same on the two sides of the Ocean, while they are altogether different on the two sides of the Tweed. It might be too much to say that the difference between England and Scotland is a difference in kind, while the difference between England and America is only a difference of degree. But if we rule both to be only differences of degree, the Scottish difference seems to me certainly the wider of the two. And of course it makes a great difference with what part of England America is compared. Rural America differs far more from rural England than urban America differs from urban England. There was nothing strange to me in the general look of the great American cities. They were very unlike York and Exeter; but they were very like Manchester and Liverpool. In short, when I landed at New York in October, my first feeling was that America was very like England; when I landed at Liverpool in April, my first feeling was that England was very like America.

III.

I said just now that I saw less difference between England and the United States than I find between England and Scotland; and that I saw one chief reason for the fact, namely, that English and Ame-

rican law are for the most part the same, while
English and Scottish law are for the most part different.   Now, on this showing, I may possibly be
asked whether I do not find a greater likeness between Ireland and either England or America than
I find between either of these lands and Scotland.
In going to Ireland, as in going to America, we
cross the sea—certainly a much smaller part of it—
and we then find ourselves in a land essentially of
our own law, while in going to Scotland we keep
within our own island, and yet find ourselves in a
land essentially of another law.   And it may happen
that more superficial likenesses between America and
Ireland may strike the British visitor to America
pretty soon after his landing.   It was an American
visitor to England who remarked—I believe he
did not complain—that in England he missed the
sound of the Irish accent.   And he who lands in
America—above all if he lands, as most of us do,
at New York—will certainly remark, whether he
welcomes or not, the sound of the Irish accent at
the very beginning of his sojourn.   Specially
will he do so if he makes, as many of us do,
his first acquaintance with dollars by spending a
large number of them on a New York hackney-
carriage.   But he may perhaps before long come to
think that the presence of English law in Ireland

and the presence of the Irish cab-driver in America
are alike phænomena which are a little abnormal,
though they may perhaps have a subtle connexion
with one another. It may be that, if English rule,
and along with it English law, had never found
their way into Ireland, the Irish cab-driver would
never have found his way to New York. And
some may even go on to think that, if the history
of mankind had taken that turn, three countries at
least would be the happier for it. Anyhow, the
likeness of the law between England and Ireland does
not bring with it the same kind of likeness between
England and Ireland which the likeness of the law
between England and America brings with it. And
the reason is plain. In Ireland English law, and all
that comes of the presence of English law, is something thoroughly foreign. In America the presence of English law, and all that comes of the presence of English law, is something thoroughly natural and native. The law of Ireland is like that of
England, because Englishmen conquered Ireland and
forced their own law upon the people of Ireland.
The law of America is like the law of England, because Englishmen, freely settling in the new land of
America, naturally took their own law with them.
But Scotland was never either conquered in the
same sense as Ireland nor settled in the same sense

as America. Scotland therefore has never accepted English law, but keeps a wholly distinct law of her own growth.

Whatever therefore of likeness the English traveller in Ireland finds between that island and his own country is due to causes exactly opposite to those which bring about the likeness between England and America. In both cases the likeness is due to the presence of Englishmen in lands beyond the bounds of England; but it is due to their presence in altogether different characters. In the one case it is the presence of conquerors in an inhabited land; in the other it is the presence of settlers in what was practically an uninhabited land. Whatever likeness there is between England and Ireland, between America and Ireland, is only on the surface. Whatever likeness there is between England and Scotland, between England and America, between America and Scotland, all belongs to the very root of the matter. The likenesses and unlikenesses are of course in all cases due to historical causes. But in the one case they are due to comparatively modern historical events, since the nations severally concerned had put on their several national characters. In the other case they are due to those subtler causes, those earlier events, which ruled that the nations concerned should severally be what they are.

I find that my feeling on this head is shared by some British travellers in America, and is not shared by others. Some say with me that the difference between England and America struck them as slight, as slighter than that between England and Scotland. On others the points of unlikeness have made more impression. Doubtless I visited America under circumstances which were likely to make me dwell on likenesses rather than on unlikenesses. It might haply have been otherwise if I had known nothing of the continent of Europe, or if I had entered America, as some have done, on its western side. But I came to America from the east, and that as a somewhat old stager in continental Europe. I came as one fresh from Italy, Greece, and Dalmatia, as one who had used his own house in England as an inn on the road between Ragusa and Boston. Among a people of the same tongue, of essentially the same laws and manners, I naturally found myself at home, after tarrying in lands which were altogether foreign. But I have no doubt that deeper causes than this would naturally lead me to seize on the most English side of everything American. To me the English-speaking commonwealth on the American mainland is simply one part of the great English folk, as the English-speaking kingdom in the European island is another part. My whole line of thought and study leads me to think, more perhaps than most men, of the everlasting ties of blood and speech, and less of the accidental separation wrought by political and geographical causes. To me the English folk, wherever they may dwell, whatever may be their form of government, are still one people. It may be that the habit of constantly studying and comparing the history of England with the history of old Greece makes it easier for me to grasp the idea of a people divided geographically and politically, but still forming in the higher sense one people. The tie that bound Greek to Greek was dearer to Kallikratidas than the advancement of Spartan interests by barbarian help. And so, to my mind at least, the thought of the true unity of the scattered English folk is a thought higher and dearer than any thought of a British Empire to the vast majority of whose subjects the common speech of Chatham and Washington, of Gladstone and Garfield, is an unknown tongue.

IV.

It may be more important to ask how far the doctrine of the essential unity of the divided branches of the English people is received by those whom it concerns on the other side of the Ocean. This is a subject on which I rather distrust my own judgement. I feel that it is a subject on which I am an enthusiast, and that my enthusiasm may possibly bias and colour any report that I may try to make. And, of course, I can give only the impressions which I have drawn from certain classes of people, impressions which may be widely different from those which another man may have drawn from other classes of people. As far as I can speak of my American acquaintances, I should say that with most of them the essential unity of the English folk is one of those facts which everybody in a sense knows, but of which few people really carry their knowledge about with them. The main facts of the case are so plain that they cannot fail to be known to every man among a people who know their own immediate and recent history so well as the Americans do. That the older American States were in the beginning English colonies, that the great mass of their inhabitants are still of English descent, that, though the infusion of foreign elements has been large, yet it is the English kernel which has assimilated these foreign elements, all these are plain facts which every decently taught man in the United States cannot fail in a certain sense to know. That is, if he were examined on the subject, he could not fail to give the right answers. But the facts do not seem to be to him living things, constantly in his mind. Those Americans with whom I have spoken, all of them without a single exception, readily and gladly accepted the statement of what I may call their *Englishry*, when it was set before them. Once or twice indeed I have known the statement come from the American side. But, though the acceptance of the doctrine was ready and glad, it seemed to be the acceptance of a doctrine which could not be denied when it was stated, but which he who accepted it had not habitually carried about in his daily thoughts. And when the statement came from the American side, it came, not as an obvious truth, but rather as the result of the speaker's own observation, as a fact which he had noticed, but which might have escaped the notice of others. I will illustrate my meaning by an incident which happened to myself. At a college dinner to which I was asked, one gentleman proposed my health in words which in everything else were most kind and flattering, but in which I was spoken of as a man of " a foreign nationality." In my answer I thanked the proposer of the toast for everything else that he had said, but begged him to withdraw one word: I was not of a foreign nationality, but of the same nationality as himself. My answer was warmly cheered, and several other speakers took up the same line. The unity of Old

and New England was in every mouth; one gentleman who had been American Minister in England
told how exactly the same thing had happened to
him at a Lord Mayor's dinner in London, how he
had been spoken of as a foreigner, and how he had
refused the name, just as I had done.

Now this story is an exact instance of what I say.
The feeling of unity between the two severed
branches is really present in the American breast,
but it needs something special to wake it up. It
comes most naturally to the Englishman of America
to speak of the Englishman of Britain as a "foreigner." The word is often so applied in American
newspapers and American books. But when the
Englishman of Britain formally rejects the name,
the Englishman of America frankly and gladly accepts the rejection, and welcomes the European
kinsman as truly one of his own house. Now I
know not how far I may judge others by myself;
but I should say that the feeling in England is
somewhat different. I do not think that Americans
are commonly thought of, or spoken of, as "foreigners." In the story that I have just told, the case
may have simply been that the Lord Mayor reckoned
the representative of the United States among
"Foreign Ministers," a formula in which the use of
the unpleasant word could hardly be avoided. It

seems to me that the American in England is welcomed above other men from beyond sea on the express ground that he is not a foreigner. Americans sometimes complain that they are welcomed indeed in England, but welcomed as if they were objects of curiosity, sometimes even that the welcome is mingled with condescension. The condescension I believe to be imaginary, a spectre called up by that spirit of touchiness of which I have already spoken. The curiosity is most real. But it is the curiosity with which we welcome a kinsman whom we have often heard of but never seen. It may sometimes take rather grotesque shapes, but it is in its essence that genuine interest which attaches to acknowledged kindred. In America it struck me that the British visitor was welcomed, kindly, cordially, hospitably welcomed, but still welcomed in the beginning as a stranger. That he is no stranger but a kinsman is a truth which dawns upon his American friends at a rather later stage. The American, it seems to me, feels a greater distinction between himself and the Englishman of Britain than the Englishman of Britain feels between himself and the American.

A good deal of this feeling is the natural result of past events, and I cannot help thinking that the result of past events has been somewhat aggravated by modern forms of speaking. The Englishman of America—he must allow me to call him so—has something to get over in acknowledging the kindred of the Englishman of Britain; the Englishman of Britain has nothing to get over in acknowledging the kindred of the Englishman of America. In the broad fact of the War of Independence there is really nothing of which either side need be ashamed. Each side acted as it was natural for each side to act. We can now see that both King George and the British nation were quite wrong; but for them to have acted otherwise than as they did would have needed a superhuman measure of wisdom, which few kings and few nations ever had. The later American war within the present century, a war which, one would think, could have been so easily avoided on either side, is a far uglier memory than the War of Independence. Still the War of Independence must be, on the American side, a formidable historic barrier in the way of perfect brotherhood. A war of that kind is something quite unlike an ordinary war between two nations which are already thoroughly formed. Two such nations can soon afford to forget, they can almost afford to smile over, their past differences. It is otherwise when one nation dates its national being—in the political sense of the word "nation"—from the defeat and humiliation of the other. If the American nation had parted off peacefully from the British nation, there would be no difficulty on either side in looking on the two English-speaking nations as simply severed branches of the same stock. The independent colony would, in such a case, find far less difficulty in feeling itself to be, though independent, still a colony, far less difficulty in feeling that all the common memories and associations of the common stock belong to the colony no less than to the mother-country. In such a case the new England might have been to the old what Syracuse, not what Korkyra, was to their common mother Corinth. But when independence was won in arms, and that by the help of foreign allies, when the very being of the new power was a badge of triumph over the old, it is not wonderful that the natural self-assertion of a new-born people often took the form of putting the past, the dependent past, as far as might be out of sight. Parents and brethren had become enemies; strangers had acted as friends; it was not wonderful if it was thought a point of honour to snap the old ties as far as might be, to take up in everything, as far as might be, the position of a new nation, rather than that of a severed branch of an old nation. I can understand that the Englishman of America may be tempted to see something of sacrifice, something like surrender of his national position, when he is called on to admit himself simply to be an Englishman of America. The Englishman of Britain has no such difficulties. To his eye the kindred lies on the surface, plain to be seen of all men. But it is not wonderful if the eye of the Englishman of America is a degree less clear-sighted. He may be pardoned if to him the kindred does not lie so visibly on the surface, if it is to him something which he gladly acknowledges when it is pointed out, but which he needs to have pointed out before he acknowledges it.

Another cause which helps to keep the mother-country and the independent colonies apart—at least in the minds of the people of the independent colonies—is the existence, and not only the existence but the near neighbourhood, of the dependent colonies of England. If Australia, Canada, South Africa, were politically as distinct from England as the United States are, I feel sure that the tie between England and the United States would be drawn much closer. As it is, there are but two independent English-speaking nations in the world; they therefore stand out in a distinct and marked opposition to each other. Were there four or five such nations, no two would stand out in this way for separate comparison; the unity among them would be far more striking than the diversity. And the United States especially would no longer have a kind of perpetual reminder of one side of the history and relations of the mother-country in the shape of a dependent colony of the mother-country on its own borders. Canada, either independent or joined to the United States, would no longer suggest thoughts which, whether they look forward or backward, are inconsistent with the full acknowledgement of the general brotherhood of the English folk.

I have applied the name English folk to all. I cannot help thinking that certain forms of speech, possibly unavoidable forms of speech, have done much to keep the two branches of the divided people asunder. The ideal after which I would fain strive would be for all members of the scattered English folk to feel at least as close a tie to one another as was felt of old by all members of the scattered Hellenic folk. Geographical distance, political separation, fierce rivalry, cruel warfare, never snapped the enduring tie which bound every Greek to every other Greek. So the Englishman of Britain, of America, of Africa, of Australia, should be each to his distant brother as were the Greek of Massalia, the Greek of Kyrênê, and the Greek of Chersôn. And, in order to compass this end, the scattered branches of the common stock must have a common name. This the old Greeks had. The Hellên remained a Hellên wherever he settled, and wherever he settled the land on which he settled became Hellas. The Greek of Attica or Peloponnêsos did not distinguish himself from the Greek of Spain by calling himself a Greek and his distant kinsman a Spaniard. But it is hard to find a name fitted in modern usage to take in all the scattered branches of the English folk. A certain class of orators on both sides of Ocean would seem to have dived into the charters of the tenth and eleventh centuries, and thence to have fished up the antiquated name of "Anglo-Saxon." We hear much big talk about the "Anglo-Saxon *race*," somewhat to the wrong of that greater Teutonic body of which Angles and Saxons are fellow-members with many others. But those who use the name most likely attach no particular meaning to it; to them it goes along with such modern creations as Anglo-Normans, Anglo-Indians, Anglo-Catholics. The very narrow historical sense of the word "Anglo-Saxon" is never thought of. It is not remembered that its use was to mark the union of Angles and Saxons under

one king, an use which naturally was forgotten as
the distinction between Angles and Saxons was
forgotten. Anyhow the name is antiquated and
affected; it is not the name which most naturally
springs to any man's lips: it is a name artificially
devised to answer a certain purpose. For the
Englishman of Britain and the Englishman of
America to greet one another as " Anglo-Saxons"
is very much as if the Greek of Peloponnèsos and
the Greek of Spain had greeted one another, not
as Hellênes, but as Danaans or Pelasgians. Yet
there certainly is a difficulty, such as the Greek
never felt, in their greeting one another by their
true name of Englishmen. So to do is easier in
Latin than in English. " Angli," " Anglici," even
" Angligenæ," might serve the turn quite well; but
the word " Englishman" has somehow got a local
meaning, as if it belonged to the soil rather than to
the stock, as if it expressed allegiance to a certain
government rather than partnership in a certain
speech and descent. Now how old is this use?
How long is it since the word " American" was
applied to English settlers in America? and how
long—a much shorter time undoubtedly—since the
word " American " was first opposed to the word
"English"? These questions belong to that large
class of questions which cannot be answered off-

hand when the answer is wanted, questions to
which the answer can be found only by keeping
them constantly in mind, and noting everything
that directly or indirectly bears upon them. In a
hymn of one of the Wesleys there is a line which
runs thus:

"The dark Americans convert."

At that line the minds of some citizens of the
United States have been known to be offended.
Yet it is certain that by "Americans" Wesley
meant only the native Indians, and I conceive that
he could not have applied the name "American"
to the English folk of any of the Thirteen Colonies.

It is yet more to be noticed that throughout
the contemporary records of the War of Independence, not only, as far as I have seen, is the word
"English" never contrasted with "American," but
the name "English" is never applied to the enemies against whom Washington and his fellows
were striving. The word which is commonly
used—which, as far as I have seen, is invariably
used—is "British." This is just as it should be;
the distinction between "American" and "British"
marks the political and geographical severance
between the English in Britain and the English in
America, without shutting out either from their

common right to the English name. Words like
"colonial," "provincial," "continental," went out of
use as the colonies ceased to be provinces, and
declared themselves to be independent states.
The new power needed a new name, and no name
more distinctive than "American" was to be
had. But "American" was still not opposed to
"English;" it was opposed to "British," as mark-
ing the severance between the English folk in
Britain and the English folk in America. We
have next to ask, When did this usage go out?
When did "English" instead of "British" come to
be the word commonly opposed to "American"?
Again we cannot answer offhand; but "British"
certainly was the word in use at the time of the
war of 1813, and I fancy that it was in use much
later. I have been told that the change took
place about the time of the Oregon disputes. I
have also been told that the change was really
brought in out of good feeling towards the mother-
country. "British" was a name which suggested
old wrongs, while no such unpleasant memories
gathered round the English name. I can neither
confirm nor deny either of these statements; but
that the change has taken place there is no doubt.
The American no longer familiarly uses the word
"British" to denote the English of Britain. As

long as he did so, his language was at least patient
of the interpretation that he still looked on himself
as an Englishman. He now habitually uses the
words "English," "Englishman," in every possible
relation, to denote the English of Britain as distinguished from himself. That is, he gives up the
English name as no longer belonging to him.
Even if the change was made out of friendli-
ness, I cannot look on it as a change for the
better. Of the two, I had rather that the Englishman of America should look on me as a brother
with whom he has a quarrel, than that he should
look on me as a stranger in blood, even though a
stranger admitted to his friendship.

It was acutely remarked to me by an American
friend that it would be easy to use the adjective
"British" according to the older usage which I had
said that I wished to see restored, but that a substantive was lacking. This is perfectly true. The
only available substantive, "Briton," will not do.
In strictness that name means a Welshman, and its
employment in that sense has gone out of use for a
much shorter time than people commonly think.
In any other use the name belongs to the same
class of names as "Anglo-Saxon." It is not the
natural name by which an Englishman speaks of
himself; it is used either in a half-laughing vein,

or because it is thought to be fine, or else of set purpose to find some name which shall take in all the people of Great Britain. Yet the only alternative would seem to be the grotesque and rather ugly form " Britisher." And I always told my American friends that I had rather be called a Britisher than an Englishman, if by calling me an Englishman they meant to imply that they were not Englishmen themselves.

Then the name " American" also suggests some questions. No one uses it now in the sense of Wesley's " dark Americans." That is, no one uses it exclusively of them. The name takes them in for some purposes, while for others it shuts them out. The word " American " for some purposes means the United States only; for some other purposes it means the whole American continent. It is certainly odd that "American languages " would be everywhere understood as meaning the native languages of the continent, while " American literature" means so much of English literature as belongs locally to the United States. To me Prescott and Motley seem as much English historians, Longfellow and Whittier seem as much English poets, as if they had been born and had written in Great Britain. They are English writers, writing in the English tongue, their own tongue,

in which they have just as much right as any native
of Great Britain. And we claim Mr. Lowell as
English also, though he did write an unpleasant
paper about "Foreigners." But in common American speech, "English literature" means the literature of the local England only. And "American
literature" seems to belong exclusively to the United
States. The phrase hardly takes in the English
literature, if there be any, of Canada; it certainly
does not take in the Spanish literature, if there be
any, of Mexico. The oddest use of all is when the
word "American" is used geographically to shut
out certain parts of the American continent. At
Niagara people talk of the "American side" and
the "English side." I suggested, "for 'American' read 'English,' and for 'English' read
'French.'" The truth is that the great land of the
United States has not yet got a name, a real local
name, like England or France, or even like Canada
or Mexico. I know not whether it is any comfort
that the lack is common to the United States of
America with the other chief confederations of the
world. The words "Switzerland" and "Swiss,"
though they had been for ages in familiar use,
never became the formal style of the Old League of
High Germany till the present century. So the
kingdom of the Netherlands, once the Seven United

Provinces, is commonly spoken of as "Holland," the name of one of its provinces only, while we commonly call its people "Dutch," the name of a great race which takes in ourselves. It is by a kindred confusion, though one which does not take exactly the same form, a confusion arising from the same lack of a real name for the country, that, when we speak of "American literature," "American institutions," "American politics," "American society," we mean the institutions, the literature, the politics, and the society, of the United States only, while by "American zoology," "American geology," etc., we mean those of the whole continent, and "American languages" distinctly excludes those languages in which alone American literature has been possible. The want of a real name for the land, and the awkwardness to which one is driven for lack of it, struck me at every turn in my American travels. The thought even sometimes occurred, What if the name of New England, a name surely to be cherished on every ground, had spread over the whole Union? It would have been better than nothing; but a real geographical name would be better still. The lack has been felt in the country itself, and somebody once proposed "Fredonia." I remember in my boyhood a map of the United States with that name on it. One may

guess that the author of the name had the words
free and *freedom* in his head ; but after what
analogy did he coin his name ? " Fredonia" quite
outdoes even the absurdity of " Secessia," of which
newspaper correspondents thought it fine to talk
twenty years back. Some one may some day make
the same attempt with a better result. Meanwhile
I see the evil, but I cannot undertake to find the
remedy by inventing a name.

<h2 style="text-align:center">V.</h2>

Now mankind are, after all, so deeply influenced
by names and formulæ that it does seem by no
means unlikely that these ways of speaking have
really had some share in keeping up and widening
the distinction between the two branches of the
English folk. They did not cause the distinction,
for they are themselves among the effects of it ;
but, in the way in which causes and effects so constantly react on one another, they may very well
have helped in sharpening the distinction and
making it more long-lived. Another cause has
perhaps had a still greater share ; namely, a growing belief that the people of the United States have
somehow lost the right—whether that right is to be
deemed a privilege or otherwise—to be looked on
as an English people. Some among them are very

anxious, strange as it seems, to make themselves
out to be a people of no particular stock, to be what
the Germans emphatically call a *Mischvolk.* Since
I have made it somewhat of my business to set
forth the essential oneness of the two great branches
of the English people, I have been met, sometimes
in friendly, sometimes in unfriendly, guise, but in
both cases in perfect seriousness, by hints that I
have forgotten the great influx of strangers, Germans and Scandinavians, for instance, into the
United States, which is supposed to have caused a
real difference of race between the English in
Britain and the English in America. I have certainly not forgotten a very obvious fact, one which
I have often insisted on, and which, when really
understood, tells my way. Those who argue in
this way forget that the phenomena of England
and America are in this matter really the same.
Since the settlement of the American colonies,
foreign settlement in England, chiefly German and
French, though certainly much smaller than in
America, has been quite large enough to be per-
ceptible. But in both cases the dominant English
element asserts its supremacy by assimilating the
stranger. Whether in Britain or in America, the
German or other foreigner becomes English; the
Englishman never becomes German. I must here

repeat some simple truths. Strict purity of blood is not to be found in any nation, and the greater part a nation plays in the history of the world, the further it is sure to be from any such purity. But in most nations there is some one element which is more than an element. There is something which is in truth the essence of the nation, the kernel round which all other elements grow, that which attracts and assimilates them all to itself. Alike in Britain and in the United States, the part of this dominant and assimilating element is played by the English stock which settled in the one land in the fifth century, in the other in the seventeenth. I am fully aware that there are parts of the United States where more German is heard than English. But there is no part of the United States where English has been supplanted by German. When any State exchanges the English speech and law for the speech and law of some other people, then I shall allow that the people of the United States are a mixed race in the sense which is intended. Till then I shall hold them to be an English people which has adopted and assimilated—just as the English of Britain have done on a somewhat smaller scale—a large infusion of strangers. Into minuter questions as to the nature of assimilation, its comparative speed and the like under different sets of circumstances, I will not now enter.

The strength of the English stock in the United States is nowhere more clearly shown than in the fact that it not only assimilates all foreign elements in those lands which were colonies of England or colonies of such colonies, but that it makes itself dominant in lands which were never settled from England, but which were settled from other European lands. The short history of New Sweden, the longer history of New Netherland, shows us the way in which one body of Teutonic settlers gave way to another, and how the various kindred elements have been fused together, but not without leaving signs of earlier diversity. In some parts of New York City, indeed, the Low-Dutch stock, whether of Holland or of England, does seem to be overshadowed by that High-Dutch infusion which sometimes veils the Hebrew. But at Albany the influence of Holland and Zealand is perfectly visible, and at Schenectady one might almost think that their High Mightinesses still ruled on both sides of the Ocean. But the lands north-west of the Ohio, above all the lands west of the Mississippi, have a yet more special history of their own, and one which tells the same lesson, in another but certainly a not less emphatic way. In the one we find a land won by Englishmen in warfare, when the colonies of England

still were provinces, from the grasp of earlier
colonists from France. In the other we find a
land which never was a possession of the British
crown, which had no part or lot in the struggle
which gave the colonies of England independence, a land to whose people Washington and
the elder Adams were men of a foreign tongue,
chiefs of a foreign nation—a land which became
part of the soil of the new English-speaking
folk, neither by warfare against the elder England
nor by settlement from the elder England, but by
bargain and sale in the days of the third President.
In the State of Missouri, in the city of St. Louis—
of the southern Louisiana which keeps its old name
I cannot speak—the name of the city at once tells
its history; and, if we look a little deeper, we soon
find signs which tell us that we are in a land which
once was French. Yet this land is now practically
English, in the sense in which the rest of the United
States are English; and in the wake of settlers of
English speech has come the usual following of
strangers, both of kindred and of foreign blood.
The elder French stock is not driven out, but it is
hidden till we specially search for it. And this
last land supplies another lesson. We have here at
once a striking parallel and a striking contrast to
some of the lands of the most famous European

Confederation. As the once Romance lands of
America revere the real Washington, who certainly
did nothing for them, so the still Romance lands of
Switzerland revere the mythical Tell, who may, at
least in a figure, be said to have done something
against them. Not only are the legendary heroes
of the Three Lands reverenced on the neutral
ground of Vaud and Geneva, they are reverenced in
Ticino itself, where the men who were so zealous
for freedom on their own soil showed themselves
only as the harshest of taskmasters. The contrast lies
in this: the Romance lands of Switzerland are Romance still; the Romance lands of America have
ceased to be Romance. The real and mythical
worthies of the elder Switzerland assuredly did nothing either for the land or the men of the Burgun-
dian and Italian cantons; but the real worthies of
the elder States of the American Union, if they did
nothing for the lands of Missouri and Louisiana,
assuredly did much for the forefathers of the great
mass of the present inhabitants of those lands.
Here are instances in which the local history of the
American States connects itself, sometimes merely
by analogy, sometimes by direct cause and effect,
with European history, and sometimes with the
oldest European history. In this way, as in so many
others, we soon come to learn that, in a land where

everything at first sight seems to be of yesterday, the past, even the very remote past, has struck its roots very deep indeed.

The English stock in the United States is thus seen to be so strong that it changes even the settlements of France into lands which are practically English. Yet there is felt to be some strangeness in applying the English name to lands which never were English in the political sense. It needs a little thought to take in that in another sense the name is strictly applicable. This is one of the cases which illustrate my general proposition, which explain why the Englishman of America is less likely to carry about with him the feeling of common brotherhood than the Englishman of Britain is, though he accepts it willingly and gladly when it is fairly set before him. The feeling in short exists unconsciously, and it shows itself unconsciously in a thousand ways. It is hardly a contradiction to say that, where the distinction between the two severed branches is most sharply and purposely drawn, the fact that it is so purposely drawn is really a witness to the real absence of any essential distinction. American interest in England seems to me to be generally as keen as any of us could wish it to be. The forms which it takes are various; some are all that we could wish them to be; others sometimes are not always so likely to lead to the result for which we are seeking.

I will here illustrate the different ways in which sometimes likeness, sometimes unlikeness, is apt to strike most strongly according to circumstances by a parallel case from travel on the European continent. An Englishman most commonly begins his travels in France, he very often begins his continental travels of any kind, with a journey in Normandy. The result of this is that he fails to see how much Normandy and England have in common. If Normandy is the first continental land that he visits, he is naturally most struck by the points of unlikeness between Normandy and England. Let him go straight on into Aquitaine, and see Normandy as he comes back, and he will at once see how much England and Normandy have in common as compared with England and Aquitaine. Now if this is true of lands speaking different tongues, it has tenfold truth between lands speaking the same tongue. Everything leads the American who visits Europe to visit England before any other part of Europe. Indeed, unless he takes special pains to chalk out some other road, he will, as a matter of course, be taken to England first of all, saving the chance of an earlier hour or two in Ireland. But I have seriously counselled American friends who

have never been in Europe, not to visit England
first. I have even counselled them, if they can
manage it—and sometimes it can be managed
—to see the less frequented parts of Europe
first, say Sicily or southern Italy, Greece or the
neighbouring lands—I dare say Spain would also
serve the turn, but I cannot speak of Spain
from my own knowledge—then to see the more
familiar lands of Italy, Germany, or France, and
to see their own mother-land last of all. One
cannot expect many American travellers to follow
this itinerary; but I believe that it would have a
very wholesome effect on any that would do so.
What I spoke of in the case of Normandy will now
come true with tenfold force. The American who
sees England first of all will naturally compare
England with his own land, and he will naturally
be most struck with points of unlikeness. If he
does not see England till he has seen other lands
where the unlikeness is far deeper, he will be most
struck with the points of likeness; he will feel himself more thoroughly at home in the land of his
fathers. It was not pleasant when I once read in
an American periodical a recommendation to American visitors to London to go somewhere or other
where they would meet only their own country-
men, and would thereby escape "the horrible Eng-

lish intonation." I do not know what "the horrible English intonation" is, and one can hardly stifle the thought that travellers who are so shocked at it had better keep on their own side of Ocean; but I cannot help thinking that, if they had first taken in their fill of lands speaking altogether strange tongues, they might have been glad to find themselves in a land where their own tongue was spoken, be the " intonation" of the speaker what it may.

VI.

With all this interest and curiosity in English matters which I found on the other side of Ocean, I was, whenever I got beyond the very first range of American minds, often struck by an amount of ignorance about English matters which I had certainly not looked for. The ignorance is indeed largely mutual, and I am certain of one thing, that the average American knows much more about his own country than the average Englishman knows about his. There certainly are plenty of people in England whose notions of American matters are passing strange. There are, for instance, not a few, fairly intelligent in many ways, who seem quite unable to grasp the most general outline of a Federal system. The relation between the States and the Union is to them a never-ending mystery. And there are some who seem, perhaps in speaking to an American visitor, to have utterly failed to grasp how large a stock of knowledge and interest such a visitor must have in common with themselves. I have known an Englishman think it needful to explain to an American lady who Sir Walter Scott was. Still I must say—even at the risk of being charged with that fault of "condescension" which of all faults I most wish to avoid—that British ignorance of America and American ignorance of Britain do not stand on the same ground. The American is really more called on to know about British matters than the Britisher is called on to know about American matters. And that for this obvious reason, that American matters cannot be thoroughly understood without constant reference to British matters, while British matters may be thoroughly understood with little or no reference to American matters. The present state of things in America implies the past history of America, and the past history of America implies the past history of England. On the other hand, the special history of America, the history of the English folk in America since the separation, though it must ever be an object of deep interest to all in the mother-land, is not in the same way part of the history of the elder England, nor is it in the same way needful for understanding the history of the elder England. I hold then that British ignorance of America is more easily to be forgiven than American ignorance of Britain. This last is largely owing to defective teaching, and I believe that the defective teaching is largely owing to a mistaken feeling of national self-assertion. The warning of Washington against meddling in the affairs of Europe was politically most sound; but Washington could hardly have meant it to be understood as forbidding all acquaintance with the past history and present state of Europe. There certainly is—I should rather say there was—a tendency in some American quarters to think and speak as if nothing can concern the American people if it be of older date than the battle of Bunker Hill, or, at any rate, older than the sailing of the Mayflower. It is doubtless a caricature when the American child, when he is asked who was the first man, is made to answer George Washington, and when, on another child suggesting Adam as a correction, the first pleads that he did not know that he was to take count of foreigners. And, when it came to this, the story should surely have gone on to say that somebody

named, not *Adam* but *Adams*, as the second man.
I am told that it is only lately that English history has been at all generally taught in any but
the highest American schools, and I fear that it
is still taught as a thing apart, not as an essential part of the history of the American people.
American children's books are sure to pay all due
honour to the Pilgrim Fathers, and, if so disposed,
to Captain John Smith of Virginia; but in the
times before Smith and the Pilgrim Fathers they
are apt to dwell more than enough on red Indians
and mastodons, and less than enough on the land
and people from which Smith and the Pilgrim
Fathers came. But it is harder still when the land
from which they came is passed by, and the rest of
the elder lands are acknowledged. A Chicago periodical told a tale of what followed when a school of
girls was set to draw a map of Europe. One girl
draws her map according to her own notions; another, by way of correction, suggests that the British islands are left out. The schoolmistress rebukes
the interference of the critic; she had not said that
there was any need to put in islands. The mortified
Britisher might thus at least have the consolation
that Sicily, Crete, and Cyprus fared no better than
his own island. This story was told in a review of
Mr. Green's "Making of England," a book which

the Chicago writer hoped might do something to
improve this state of things. But, more seriously,
I was struck, often in quarters where I should hardly
have looked for it, with what seemed to me a strange
ignorance of English matters, especially of English
geography. I was amazed, for instance, to be
asked whether Lincolnshire was on the west side of
England or the east—to be asked, and that by a
scholar of œcumenical fame, in what part of England Northamptonshire lay—and, cruellest of all, to
be asked in very intelligent company whether the
county of Somerset was called from the dukes of
Somerset. That was indeed an unkind blow to an
immemorial Teutonic *gá*, to fancy it called after
some Seymour of yesterday, or even after one of
the somewhat older Beauforts.* I need not say
that Madison County, Tompkins County, and the
like, was what was in the speaker's mind. Now I
shall of course be asked whether an Englishman on
the same level would know any more of the geography of America. And I will say beforehand that,
if I have been amazed in America at ignorance
of the geography of England, I have often been

---

* I cannot help putting on record, as one of the curiosities of
criticism, that a New York paper fancied that what I complained of in telling this story was "ignorance of the history
of an English ducal family."

just as much amazed in England at the ignorance of
the geography of continental Europe. But as for
English knowledge of American geography, it seems
to me that a decently educated Englishman ought
to know the position of great and renowned States
like Virginia and Massachusetts, but that he may
be forgiven for knowing very little about Arizona
and Colorado, beyond the fact that they lie a long
way.west of Virginia and Massachusetts. But then
all England, every corner of it, is, not as Arizona
and Colorado, but as Virginia and Massachusetts,
and something more. For no part of Britain or of
Europe looks to Virginia or Massachusetts as a
mother-land. But every corner of England is, or
may prove to be, the parent or the metropolis of
this or that corner of America. The Federal capital bears the name of the patron hero, and the
patron hero bore the name which his forefathers
took from one or other of the obscure Washingtons
in England. Such an instance as this is typical. I
think we may reasonably expect an American of
average thought and average knowledge to know
more of English geography and of everything English than we can expect the Britisher on the same
level to know of American matters, or than we can
expect men of different European nations to know
of each other's lands. In none of the other cases is

the land which a man knows or of which he is ignorant the direct, obvious, acknowledged, cradle of
his own people.

I have to put in some modifying adjectives,
lest I should be met with an answer out of my
own mouth. In England I have ever preached
the lesson "antiquam exquirite matrem," while in
America I have, at the expense of metre, preached
it in the shape of " antiquiorem exquirite matrem."
I am not likely to forget that, if the English
settlements in America are colonies of the English
settlements in Britain, so the English settlements
in Britain are themselves colonies of the older
English land on the European mainland. In the
wider history of the three Englands no fact is of
greater moment; it is in fact the kernel, almost
the essence, of their whole history. Still the
constant acknowledgement and carrying about of
that fact is a kind of counsel of perfection which
every one cannot be expected to bear in mind.
The analogy between the English settlement in
Britain and the English settlement in America is
real, but it is hidden. The points of unlikeness
lie on the surface. The far longer time of separation between the first England and the second,
the consequences following on that longer separation, above all the far wider break in the matter

of language and institutions—to say nothing of the original diversity in date and circumstances between the settlements of the sixth century and the settlements of the seventeenth—all these things join together to make the relations between the first England and the second altogether unlike the relations between the second England and the third. The oldest England on the European continent should never be forgotten by the men of the middle England in the isle of Britain. But it never can be to them all that the middle England in the isle of Britain surely ought to be to the men of the newest England on the mainland of America.

VII.

The main ties between the mother-country and her great colony are those which are always likely to be the main results of community of stock; that is, community of language and community of law. I will speak first of language. And here I must fall back on my former saying, what some think my former paradox, that the difference between England and Scotland seemed to me greater than the difference between England and America. I may add that the difference in each case is, to a great extent, a difference of the same kind. And here I must venture on a further paradox. The difference between Scotland and England and the difference between America and England is, I hold, largely owing to the fact that both Scotland and America are in many things more English than England itself. This is above all things true in the matter of language. People talk of "Americanisms" and of "Scotticisms," as if they were in all cases corruptions, or at all events changes, introduced by Americans and Scotsmen severally into the existing English tongue. Now I do not deny that there are a good many "Americanisms" and a few "Scotticisms" which really answer that definition. But I maintain that the great mass of both classes come under quite another head. What people commonly call an "Americanism" or a "Scotticism" is, for the more part, some perfectly good English word or phrase, which has gone out of use in England, but which has lived on in America or in Scotland. To take two very obvious instances, most people, I feel sure, would call *bairn* a Scotch word ; most people, I feel sure, would call *fall*, in the sense of *autumn*, not indeed an American word, but an American use of the word. It almost seems as if they believed that the use of the word *bairn* in any sense, and the use of the word *fall* in that particular sense, was something that the Scots and

the Americans severally had devised of their own
hearts, and in which England never had any share
at any time. Yet nothing is more certain than
that *bairn* is Scotch only in the sense that it has
gone out of use in England, but has lived on in
Scotland. West-Saxon Alfred talks about his
"bairns," while the word would certainly not have
been understood by any true Scottish Kenneth or
Malcolm. So it is with "mickle;" so it is with a
crowd of other words which are commonly set
down as "Scotch," but which are not, except in
modern usage, even distinctly Northern. *Fall*, in
the particular sense of autumn, is, in the like sort,
American only in the sense that it has lived on in
America while it has gone out of use in England.
Or one should rather say only that it has gone
out of use in high-polite speech in England. I
can distinctly remember the phrase "spring and
fall" in my childhood, and the good old word still
abides in the popular speech of many districts,
perhaps of all. So does "rare," in the sense of
underdone meat, a sense which has nothing whatever to do with Latin "rarus." When I first heard
it in the American use it really puzzled me,
but I was presently ashamed to learn that it
was to be daily heard on the lips of my nearest
neighbours. "Scotch" in common talk never

means the Gaelic speech of the true Scots; the
word always means the speech of that part of
Northern England which came under the rule of
the kings of the true Scots. The English of that
district was naturally less affected than Southern
English by the Norman and French influences of
the eleventh, twelfth, and thirteenth centuries.
It therefore keeps a crowd of good and strong
English words which have dropped out of use
in Southern English. On the other hand, the
later connexion between France and Scotland,
and the respect shown in Scotland to the Roman
law, have brought in a good many French and
Latin words which are unknown in Southern
English. Thus the Northern and Southern forms
of English parted asunder, and the speakers of the
Southern form have come to apply the name
"Scotch" not only to the really distinctive characteristics of the Northern form, but to those cases
in which something which was once common to
both forms has lived on in the Northern form only.

Something of the same kind has happened to
the English language as spoken in the United
States. In the matter of language, as in most
other matters, the United States have followed the
usual law of colonies. A colony is always exposed
to two opposite tendencies, which, though opposite,

are found not uncommonly to work busily side by side. There is a greater tendency to stand still, and there is also a greater tendency to go ahead, than there is in the mother-country. A colony which has no chance of going ahead is likely to stand very still indeed, much stiller than an old country. A small isolated colony, say a small island, is likely to become one of the most old-world places that can be. It will in many things keep on the state of things which existed in the mother-country at the time of the settlement, long after that state of things has, in the mother-country itself, become a thing of the past. It has become a proverb that, if you wish to see old France, you must go to French Canada. And for many things, if you wish to see old England, you must go to New England. In the United States the tendency to go ahead has certainly reached as great a development as in any part of the world; but it has by no means driven out the opposite tendency to stand still. I need not say that I noticed many things in which our kinsfolk beyond the Ocean had —sometimes, I thought, for good, sometimes, I thought, for evil—left us behind. But I also noticed some things in which they had—sometimes, I thought, for good, sometimes for evil—lagged behind us. There is a vast deal of conservative feeling, or at least of conservative habit, at work in the United States, at any rate in the older States. There is much about them in speech, in manners, in institutions, which has a thoroughly old-world character, much that has lived on from the England of the seventeenth century, much in which the circumstances of the settlers called back into being things far older than the England of the seventeenth century. In short, according to the general doctrine with which I set out, when anything that seems strange to a British visitor in American speech or American manners is not quite modern on the face of it, it is pretty certain to be something which was once common to the older and the newer England, but which the newer England has kept, while the older England has cast it aside. And it is not very hard to distinguish between usages which have this venerable sanction and usages which have come in only yesterday. It does not need any very great effort to discern between words, phrases, ways of looking at things, which have been handed on from the days of John Smith of Virginia or Roger Williams of Rhode Island, and words, phrases, ways of looking at things, which have come in under the reign of the stump-orator, the interviewer, and that deadliest of all foes to the English tongue and to every other tongue, the schoolmaster.

I have drawn a parallel between the Scottish
and the American forms of English; but it is a
parallel which is far from holding good in every
point. The Scottish—that is, the Northern—
form of English is, in the strictest sense, a dialect.
That is to say, it is an independent form of the
language, which might have come to set the
standard of the language and to become the polite
and literary speech, instead of that form of the
language to which that calling actually fell. Or
rather, as long as Scotland was politically distinct
from the southern England, the Northern form of
English actually did set the standard within its
own range. It was the polite and literary speech
within the English-speaking lands of the Scottish
kings. It is only the political union of the king-
doms which has brought Northern English down
from that place of dignity, and has caused
Southern English to set the standard of speech
through the whole of Great Britain. Whatever
a Scotsman may speak, he now writes after the
manner of a southern Englishman. But the
Englishman of America does not write—he is in
no way called on to write—after the manner of
the Englishman of Britain, but after his own
manner. For his manner of speech, however it
may differ from the speech of the Englishman of

Britain, does not differ as a dialect strictly so called. And this is none the less true, though it is quite certain that several dialects of English are spoken in America. Some Americans, specially curious in such matters, profess to mark some difference of speech in almost every State, and to be able in most cases to say from what State a man comes. To this amount of discernment I naturally can make no claim; but I can see some marked points of difference between the speech of the Northern and Southern States, taken as wholes. And I can further see that the speech of Virginia agrees in some points with the speech of Wessex, points in which it differs from the speech of either Boston. Thus, for instance, the surname *Carter*—a surname which to us does not sound specially patrician, but which in Virginia is reckoned to be at least as noble as Berkeley, if not as Montmorency—is locally sounded *Kyartah.* Now if the utterance of the latter half of the word may seem to be that of a London lounger, the utterance of the former half is genuine West-Saxon, whether of the days of Alfred or the days of Victoria. But if we come to compare the English of the United States as a whole with the English of Britain as a whole, there is no difference of dialect strictly so called between them. There is not the same kind

of difference which there is between the English of
the Northern and Southern parts of Britain itself.
The test seems to lie in the fact which I have just
spoken of. The speaker of Northern English finds
it needful to adopt, for certain purposes, the Southern form of English, instead of that which is natural to him. But no American speaker or writer
ever thinks it needful to adopt the British form of
his own language, any more than a British speaker
or writer thinks it needful to adopt the American
form.

And yet it is perfectly plain that the English
tongue common to Britain and America is not
spoken and written in exactly the same way in
Britain and in America. The man of either land
carries with him marks characteristic of his own
land which will not fail to bewray him to men of
the other land. But those marks are not of the
nature of dialectic difference strictly so called. I
told my American hearers, in some of the lectures
which I gave in several places, that between them
and us I could see no difference of language, no
difference of dialect, but that there was a considerable difference of local usage. Now local usage in
matter of speech, whether it be of old standing or
of quite modern origin, is altogether another thing
from real difference of dialect. Difference of dia-

lect is a matter which lies pretty much beyond the
control of the human will. It is often unconscious,
it is almost always involuntary; if any reason can
be given for the difference, it is a reason which
does not lie on the surface, but which needs to be
found out by philological research. But mere local
usage, though it may have become quite immemorial, is not thus wholly beyond our own control.
There is something conscious about it, something
at any rate which can be changed by an immediate
act of the will. For mere difference of local usage in
language we can often give some very obvious reason which needs no philological research at all. For
instance, what we may call the language of railways
is largely different in England and in America.
But this is no difference of dialect, only difference
of local usage. In each case a particular word has
been chosen rather than another. In each case the
word which has been chosen sounds odd to those
who are used to the other. In each case we can
sometimes see the reason for the difference of
usage, and sometimes not. No obvious reason can
be given why in England we speak of the "rail-
way," while in America they commonly speak of
the "rail*road*." But no one on either side can
have the least difficulty in understanding the word
which is used on the other side. And indeed the

American may say that, in this as in some greater and older matters, he has stuck to the older usage. Though "rail*road*" is now seldom used in England, my own memory tells me that it was the more usual name when the thing itself first came in. "Rail*way*," for what reason I know not, has displaced "rail*road*" in England, and it is worth remarking that it is doing the same in some parts of America. Here one can see no reason for one usage rather than the other, and no advantage in one usage rather than the other. But when the American goes on to speak, as he often does, of the railroad simply as "the road," his language may sometimes be a little misleading, but it is easy to see the reason for it. In England we had everywhere roads before we had railroads; the railroad needed a qualifying syllable to distinguish it from the older and better known kind of road. But in a large part of America the railroad is actually the oldest road; there is therefore no such need to distinguish it from any other. To us this seems rather like a state of things in which printing should be familiar, but writing unknown; but it is a state of things which the circumstances of our time have brought about in a large part of the United States. That is to say, the two tendencies of which I spoke have been at work side by side. The tendency to lag behind has hindered the growth of a good system of roads; the tendency to go ahead has brought in a gigantic system of railroads. Here we see the reason for the different use of language. We see it also in the different names for the thing which, when the railroad is made, runs along its rails. In Britain it is, at least in the language of travellers, a "carriage;" in America it is a "car." This at least is by no means a distinction without a reason. The different forms of English railway-carriage might afford some curious matters for observation to a philosopher of the school of Mr. Tylor. Nowhere can the doctrine of survivals be better studied. The original railway-carriage was the old-fashioned carriage or coach put to a new use; the innovation lay in putting several such carriages together. It is only quite gradually that what we may call a picture of the old carriage has disappeared from our trains. This is as distinct a survival as the useless buttons on a modern coat which once fastened up a lappet, helped to carry a sword, or discharged some other useful function now forgotten. And a further survival remains in technical speech; what the traveller by railway calls a "carriage," the railway official still calls a "coach." But the American "car" was not made after any such pattern as the English coach. It

is strictly a "car;" at any rate it is quite unlike
the special meaning attached to the word "carriage." If anything other than itself was present
to the mind of the deviser of the American car, it
was rather the cabin of a steamer than any earlier
kind of carriage; and such an origin is suggested
by the American phrase of being "on board" a
train, which I fancy is never heard in England.
Among European things, the older kind of American car is most like that which is used on the
Swiss railways, as if there were some kind of
federal symbolism in both. And now another form
of the American car is making its way into England, and with the thing the name comes too. For
"car" then there is a good reason; but it is hard
to see why a railway-station should be called a
"depôt." The word "station" is not etymologi-
cally English; it is therefore not so good a name
as the German *bahnhof*; but it is quite naturalized
and familiar, while "depôt" is still foreign, and
hardly becomes less so by being sounded as if it
were Italian and written *dipo*. But on several
American railroads the name is beginning to give
way to the more reasonable word "station."

All these instances taken from railway matters
are necessarily very modern; I will take another
which I have no doubt is as old as English settle-

ment in America. In England we use the word
"shop" both for a place where things are made or
done and for a place where things are sold. In
America the word is confined to the place where
things are made or done, as " barber-shop," "car-
penter-shop;" a place where things are sold is a
"store." Less old most likely, but certainly not of
yesterday, is the usage which confines the name
" corn" to one particular kind of corn—that, namely, which we know as " Indian corn," or maize. I
heard a most distinguished Englishman—Britisher,
at all events—lecture to an American audience on
the history of the English corn-laws; and I doubted
in my own mind whether all his hearers would understand that he was speaking of wheat. Now
neither of these forms of speech comes among the
cases in which the colony has kept on the elder
usage of the mother-country. This hardly needs
proof in the case of " corn." But the narrower use
of that word is exactly analogous to the narrower
use of the word " beast " among English graziers,
and of the word " bird " among English sportsmen.
In the case of " shop," the word is perfectly good
English both in the wider and in the narrower sense,
as it is in a good many other senses besides. But I
cannot find that " store" was ever used in England
in the American sense, till it came in quite lately

in the case of " co-operative stores."   But a perfectly good reason for the difference of usage can be found in some circumstance of early colonial life. In the early settlements a shop was really a " store," in a sense in which it hardly is now on either side of Ocean. And the " co-operative store" may be so called for some reason of the same kind, or it may be because the name is thought to be finer, or it may be a mere transplantation of the American name. The " shop" or the " store" suggests its contents ; and I dare say that there is some good reason, though I do not see it, why the contents of one particular kind of " store" should be specially called " dry goods." The contents of some other kinds of store seem to the untechnical mind to be equally dry. But the phrase, however it arose, is just like our phrase " hardware," which does not take in all things that are in themselves hard. Then, again, I have known some foolish Britishers mock at such phrases as " town lot," " city lot ;" but these are perfectly good and natural names for things to which we have nothing exactly answering in modern England. The constant use of the word " block," in showing a man his way about a town, struck me at first as odd. But it is a perfectly good use. American towns are built in blocks, in a way in which the elder English towns are not. Yet

something very like American "blocks" may be
seen in the town of Winchelsey, laid out for building, but only partly built, in the days of Edward the
First. The "city lot" suggests the "city" itself, of
which we certainly hear much more in America
than in England. The history of the word "city" in
England is rather strange. At some time later than
Domesday and earlier than Henry the Eighth, it
came to be confined on one hand and extended on
the other, so as to take in all places that were
bishops' sees, and no places that were not. In
America a "city" means what we should call a corporate town or municipal borough. But in England the word "city" is seldom used, except either
in rather formal speech or else to distinguish the
real city of London from the other parts of the
"province covered with houses" which in common
speech bears its name. In America the word "city"
is in constant use, where we should use the word
"town," even though the place spoken of bears the
formal rank of a city. I remember getting into
strange cross-purposes with an American gentleman
who, in speaking of a visit to London, went on
speaking of "the city," when he meant parts of the
province covered with houses far away from what I
understood by that name. "Town," in New England at least, has another meaning. A "town" or

"township" may contain a "city" or it may not.
On the other hand, one often hears the phrase
"down town," even in New York itself. New
York, by the way, calls itself a "metropolis;" in
what sense of the word it is not easy to guess, as it
can hardly be because it is, along with Baltimore
and several other cities, the seat of a Roman Catholic archbishopric. To take an example from quite
another line of life, I was struck with the use of
"first name" for "Christian name." It may have
come in out of tenderness to Baptists and Quakers,
to say nothing of Jews. Yet it sounds as if
it were older; it sounds, so to speak, "pilgrim-
fatherly;" yet, if so, it is not easy to understand,
as the Pilgrim Fathers surely practised infant
baptism.

All these are examples of those differences,
not in language but in the local use of language,
which naturally grew up through difference of
place and circumstances. In these there is no
corruption of language; we can hardly say that
there is any change of language. There is no real
dialectic difference; though some of them have
thus much in common with dialectic differences
that they have come of themselves without any fixed
purpose, even though we often can, which we cannot in the case of strictly dialectic difference, see

why they have come. It is otherwise when one
word is used rather than another under the notion
of its being finer. This is plainly the case with
"depôt," and I suppose it is also with "conductor"
for "guard." But one cannot see either that "railroad" is finer than "railway," or that "railway" is
finer than "railroad." If "store" may, from one
point of view, be thought finer than "shop," the
increased fineness is quite accidental; it is another
thing when any man on either side calls his shop or
store his "establishment." In nearly all these
cases the difference matters nothing to one whose
object is to save some relics of the good old English tongue. One way is for the most part as good
as the other; let each side of the Ocean stick to its
own way, if only to keep up those little picturesque
differences which are really a gain when the substance is essentially the same. This same line of
thought might be carried out in a crowd of phrases,
old and new, in which British and American usage
differs, but in which neither usage can be said to be
in itself better or worse than the other. Each usage
age is the better in the land in which it has grown
up of itself. A good British writer and a good
American writer will write in the same language
and the same dialect; but it is well that each
should keep to those little peculiarities of estab-

lished and reasonable local usage which will show on which side of the Ocean he writes.

On the other hand, besides unavoidable dialectic difference, besides reasonable difference in local usage, there is such a thing as distinct abuse and corruption of language. Our common tongue certainly suffers a good deal in this way on both sides of the Ocean. If good English is common to both sides, bad English takes characteristic forms on each side; and unluckily, each side often finds it easier to copy the abuses of the other than to stick to the noble heritage which is common to both. Each too often copies the slang of the other side, both the philosophic and the vulgar slang. To the former class both sides certainly contribute; "racial" I believe is American; but "sociology" is undoubtedly British. As for purely vulgar slang, it is perhaps hardly worth while trying to find out which land outdoes the other. Possibly the go-ahead side of the younger English land may have won for it the first place. Or it may merely be that slang comes to the front in America in some ways that it does not in England. Newspaper language in England has certainly fallen very low; still English newspapers of any position do not indulge in mere slang in the same way as the American papers which most nearly answer to them. But I do not think that a

cultivated American gentleman deals more in slang
than a British gentleman of the same class. And
after all, it is not easy to define slang, though
we commonly know it when we hear it. Slang,
I should think, was always conscious in its origin. A word or phrase is used, not unconsciously under the natural compulsion of some good
reason for its use, but consciously, indeed of set
purpose, because it is thought to sound fine or
clever. It presently comes to be used by crowds of
people as a matter of course, without any such
thought; but its origin sticks to it; it remains
slang; it never becomes the true yoke-fellow of
words and phrases which have grown up of themselves as they were really needed. Or again, there
may be a word or phrase which is good enough in
its turn with others, but which, if used constantly
to the exclusion of others, seems to partake of the
nature of slang. Some favourite American forms of
speech seem to us in this way to savour of slang, and
I believe that some favourite British forms of speech
in the like sort savour of slang to an American. To
take a very small example, perhaps the better because it is so very small, the word "certainly" is a
very natural form of granting any request; but in
England we should hardly use it except in granting
a request of some little importance, or one about

the granting of which there might be some little doubt; American use extends it to the very smallest civilities of the table. In the same way there are American uses of the words "like" and "believe" which to us seem odd. I have heard a man, when offered some small matter of meat or drink, say that he *believed* he could not take any. But I am not sure that this is slang; and the peculiar use of "like"—"I felt *like* to do it," meaning, "I felt a wish or a call to do it"—is itself like to be good usage and not slang. To "loan," as a verb, has to us a strange sound, and the verb "to rent" seems to be used in exactly the opposite meaning to what it bears in England. But "loan," though an abuse of speech, is not exactly slang, and "rent" may refer to some point of usage. But "I guess" I have always stood up for, as a perfectly good form, if only it is not always used to the exclusion of other forms. "I reckon" is as good English as English can be; it is only at "I calculate" that one would begin to kick; but I do not think that "I calculate" is often heard in the kind of American society to which I was used. It might, however, be taken as an instance of the way in which technical and special words get into common use, sometimes on one side of the Ocean, sometimes on the other, and which seem odd to those who are not used to them. Let me tell an Oxford tale of perhaps five-and-thirty years ago. A story was told in a common-room of an American clergyman who was in the habit of getting into theological discussions with his bishop, and who was sometimes a little puzzled as to the way in which he ought to behave in such cases towards his spiritual superior. "I had a respect for his office," said the presbyter; "but I did not like to *endorse* all that he said." A fit of laughter went round the room. Thirty-five years ago there seemed something irresistibly ludicrous in applying a commercial word like "endorse" to agreement or disagreement on a theological matter. I am quite sure that no one would laugh at it now either in America or in Britain; we all endorse, or decline to endorse, positions on all questions, theological, political, philosophical, or any other. But I doubt whether any one in England would talk of "the balance of the day," a phrase which I have heard of in America, though I should doubt its being common. Purely legal phrases, too, seem to get more easily into common use in America than here, and I am told that the same is the case with medical phrases also. I was a good deal amazed at first to see "Real Estate," "Real Estate Office," written up as the mark of a place of business. I knew my Blackstone well enough to have no difficulty as to what was meant; but it looked to me very much as if somebody had advertised a "Jetsam and Flotsam Office." But I presently found that "real estate," "to buy real estate," were phrases in daily use, both in the newspapers and in common talk. Now certainly no one in England would, if a man had bought houses or lands, say that he had bought "real estate." We should, if we did not define the particular thing bought, be more likely to veil it under the general name of "property."

The names of things lead not unnaturally to the names of places. The art of naming places, like the art of making prayers, seems to be one of the lost arts. In an old country there is but little room for its exercise; and, when we do make an attempt, our attempts are seldom lucky. In a new country it has to be tried every day. I was going to say that in the United States the art had steadily gone down; and so for a long time it certainly did; but I am not sure that the worst is not past. In an extempore discourse which I was called on to give on Washington's birthday, I tried to show how much of American history a man versed in European history, but knowing nothing of America, might make out by simply noting the local nomenclature along the Eastern coast. He would see, from names like Boston, Plymouth, Bristol, and a crowd of others,

that the land had been mainly colonized from England. But names like Haarlem and Staten Island,
even if he did not light on the fact that New York
had once been New Amsterdam, would teach him
that there had been settlements from the Netherlands also. Among the English names, he might
make guesses, right or wrong, as to the reasons why
the names of such and such English places were reproduced. Boston would most likely put him on
a right scent and Plymouth on a wrong one.
Names like Charles River, James Town, Maryland,
Carolina, might help him to the general date of the
settlements. And, once put on this tack, he might
possibly even be led to make some inferences from
a comparison between the nomenclature of the
northern and of the southern parts of the land
which he was surveying. He might remark that
names taken from royal personages in Europe are
much thicker in the South, while in the North he
would come across more names of that peculiar
character of which Salem and Providence are examples. He might not unfairly guess that this
difference betokened something as to the political
and religious character of the different settlements.
He might not unreasonably hold that he had lighted
on Cavaliers at one end and on Puritans at the
other. And, in the land between the two, he

might guess that such a name as Philadelphia was not given without a reason. And that reason could hardly be that the American Philadelphia stood to Philadelphia in Asia in the same relation in which the American Boston and Haarlem might reasonably be thought to stand to Boston and Haarlem in Europe. But what would he make of the name of the federal capital? Boston, Haarlem, Plymouth, Bristol, are all places after which younger settlements might reasonably be called. But why should anybody call any place, above all why should anybody call the capital of a great confederation, after places so utterly obscure as either of the Washingtons of the old world? I really think that an ingenious man might hit on the true explanation without any knowledge of the fact. Many places are called after men, and many men are called after places. It would really be a natural inference that a place-name otherwise so hard to account for as that of Washington was due to the place being called in honour of a man who had the good luck to bear the name of one of the older and less famous Washingtons in the mother-land.

I say "good luck," because it was good luck indeed that the father of his country bore the honest name of an English village, keeping on the memory of a Teutonic *gens* and its eponymous hero. Fancy if the first President had borne the name of the second or of the third, or indeed of any of his successors till the name of Lincoln became more famous as the name of one of the leaders of men than it had ever been as the name of an illustrious Roman and Danish city. I could not venture to carry my imaginary inquirer far from the Eastern coast. His stock of inferences would soon fail him; he would soon be utterly puzzled and baffled. There is no greater contrast than between the older and newer nomenclature of American towns. The older names fall into three or four rational and intelligible classes which have a history and a meaning.. There are the Indian names, whether names of districts or of particular places. Massachusetts keeps its name in the newer England, exactly as Kent keeps its name in the elder England. Then there are the various classes of English names, names of places in England, names of persons, descriptive names, like Long Island—fellow to Greek Makris—and devotional names, answering to the Poseidonia and Artemisia of the Greek, and to the Wodensborough, the Thundersley, and the Freysthorp, of the heathen days of England. All these are thoroughly good and reasonable. And equally good and reasonable are the names which have lived on from the settlements of other Euro-

pean nations, Haarlem, St. Louis, New Orleans;
pity, I should say, that New Amsterdam and Fort
Orange ever yielded to New York and Albany.
Only in this last case that very amusing book, "The
Memoirs of an American Lady," could never have
given us those vivid pictures of the manners and
customs of a folk of "Albanians" who had no part
or lot in Scanderbeg or Ali Pasha. But alongside
of all these thoroughly respectable and rational
names, what are we to say to the wild nomenclature
of many places of later origin? Chicago indeed
keeps its Indian name; Springfield in Illinois is as
rational as Springfield in New England; Buffalo,
though there is something comic about the sound,
may be allowed to pass as descriptive. Buffalo,
according to the teaching of zoology, is near akin to
Cowbridge, if not to Oxford, and the form of the
word did not allow the ending to be so easily added.
But what are we to say to those namers of places
who, with such a stock of good Teutonic endings,
seem to have scorned them all, or not to have
known that they were endings? Why, with *-ton*
and *-burgh* and *-wick* and *-thorp*, and Danish *-by* for
the Scandinavian settlers, all to choose from—why
is French *ville* to be stuck·to the end of plain English names? *Varietyville* is at least consistent; the
ending is not worse than the beginning; it hangs

together better than *Mechanicsburg,* where the ending is so much better than the beginning. But why *Westville,* when it would have been so easy to say *Weston* or *Westbury?* I confess that it provoked me into saying that, if I had to coin a *gentile* for the people of Westville, I could call them nothing but the *Westvillains. Owensborough* and *Evansville,* not very far apart on the map, suggest that a wise and a foolish Briton must have pitched their tents in the same quarter of the world. Why again *Whitneyville,* when *Whitney* is a good place-name ready made? And, more fearful still, I believe it is a fact that the United States, besides many Washingtons, contain a *Washingtonville.* In these names given from men—for Whitneyville was of course called from Whitney as a surname—there is often a certain helplessness. We get Madison, Columbus, even Adams, without any ending at all. Or sometimes " city" is not so much stuck on as put alongside, as in Jefferson City, as if the name-givers had been agglutinative Turks or Huns who had not reached the art of inflexion. Then, while it is perfectly reasonable to call an English place Boston, a Dutch place Haarlem, and a French place New Orleans, no good reason surely can be found for Athens, Memphis, Troy, Cairo, places which certainly do not claim a metropolis in any of their older namesakes, and which do not convey the same historical and moral lesson as Philadelphia. But the strangest display of all is to be found in a certain district of the State of New York, over which I heard it wittily said that a governor whose name I have forgotten had shaken out his Lemprière. Half the cities of antiquity are reproduced, and not only the cities, but the men. There is not only *Ithaca*, now memorable as the seat of a famous University; not far off there is *Ulysses*. Homer, Ovid, and a crowd of others appear on the map, and in a gathering of records I saw the act of the State Legislature " for the incorporation of the village of *Manlius*." Where Troy is, Rome does not fail to follow; and there is a newspaper called "The Roman Sentinel," of which I ventured to ask whether the papers on the other side ever spoke of it as "the Goose." Nor is the founder of Rome absent; it may even be that some notion of the manner of life of the true Roman peeps out in the fact that on the railroad the next station to *Romulus* is *Farmer*. In other cases too there seemed some approach to fitness in the name chosen. Geneva is at least on a lake; Syracuse stands on a bay of a lake in which I tried to see some likeness to the great harbor. Syracuse indeed must have some kind of consciousness of its own being. As the elder Syracuse on fitting days shouts loudly for " Santa Lucia," so the younger, when I passed by it on October 31, was keeping " Saint Lucy's fair." In the names of counties it is odd that the English *shire* has, as in Ireland, so utterly given way to the French name. Where by any chance it exists, it seems not to be understood. There is a Berkshire in Pennsylvania, and its chief town is Reading; but one sees it spoken of as " Berkshire co.," as one has heard people—not natives—speak of the *Bargate* at Southampton. Even in Massachusetts, one has to record the frightful fact that Norfolk and Suffolk are put the wrong way on the map. Yet even this is not worse than when, nearer home, the county of Tipperary was divided into *ridings* (*trithings*), and the number of them was two.

In pronunciation strictly so called, I mean the utterance of particular words as distinguished from any general tone, accent, intonation, or the like, I remarked less difference between America and England than I did in the use of the words themselves. Of certain dialectic differences within the United States themselves I have already said something. When the Virginian says " doe" and " floe" for " door" and " floor," it is as truly a case of dialect in the strictest sense as the difference between the

dialect of Somerset and the dialect of Yorkshire.
But I noticed some prevalent differences of pronunciation in America which were in no sense dia-
lectical, but which were clearly adopted on a principle. I fancy that something that may be called a
principle has more influence on pronunciation in
America than it has in England. This remark is
not my own ; I found it, or something to the same
effect, in an American periodical. It was there remarked that in America there is a large class of
people who read a great deal without much education, and who are apt to draw their ideas of pronunciation rather from the look of the words in the
book than from any traditional way of uttering
them. One not uncommonly comes across people
of this kind in England, and everything is likely to
make the class larger in America. This will most
likely account for some cases, specially for one on
which I shall have something to say presently. But
there are other cases in which the American usage,
though it sounds odd to a British ear, is strictly
according to the analogy of the English tongue. I
heard in America "ópponent" and "ínquiry," and
very odd they sounded. But they simply follow
the English rule of throwing the accent as far back
as we can, without regard to the Latin or Greek
quantity. If we say "théatre"—which, by the

way, is accidentally right, according to the Greek *accent*—"aúditor," "áblative," and a crowd of other words of the same kind, we may as well say "ópponent" and "ínquiry." The only reason against so doing is, I suppose, that they are a little hard to say, which is doubtless the reason why, while everybody says "aúditor" and "sénator," nobody says "spéctator." But there is one word on which I wish to speak a little more at large, as a clear instance in which the schoolmaster or the printed text or some other artificial influence has brought about a distinct change in pronunciation. The word "clerk" is in England usually sounded "clark," while in America it is usually sounded "clurk." I say "usually," because I did once hear "clurk" in England, and because I am told that in some places the sound is not uncommon. On the other hand, I was told at Philadelphia that some old people there still said "clark," and—a most important fact—that those who said "clark" also said "marchant." Now it is quite certain that "clark" is the older pronunciation, the pronunciation which the first settlers must have taken with them. This is proved by the fact that the word as a surname— and it is one of the commonest of surnames—is always sounded, and most commonly written, "Clark" or "Clarke." In England I believe this

spelling is universal. I suspect that "Clerk" as a
surname, so spelled, is distinctively "Scotch," in
the modern sense of that word. Again, in writers
of the sixteenth and early seventeenth century, the
word itself is very often written "clark" or "clarke."
But of course "clerk" was at all times the more
clerkly spelling, as showing the French and Latin
origin of the word. It is plain therefore that the
pronunciation "clurk" is not traditional, but has
been brought in artificially, out of a notion of
making the sound conform to the spelling. But
"clurk" is no more the true sound than "clark;"
the true sound is "clairk," like French "clerc."
"Clark" and "clurk" are both mere approximations to the French sound, and "clark" is the
older, and surely the more natural, approximation.
The Scotsman who writes his surname "Clerk"
assuredly does not call himself "Clurk," any more
than he follows us Southrons in degrading "Perth"
into "Purth." The truth is that we cannot
sound "clerk" as it is spelled; that is, we cannot
give the *e* before *r* the same sound which we
give it when it is followed by any other consonant. We on this side cannot do it when *r* is
followed by another consonant; and the not uncommon sound of "Amurrica" as the name of the
western continent seems to show that there is some

difficulty in sounding it, even when *r* stands by itself. We cannot sound *e* in "clerk" exactly as we
sound *e* in "tent." This explains the history of a
crowd of words, some of Teutonic, some of Latin
origin, in which the spelling is *e*, but in which the
sound has, just as in "clerk," fluctuated between *a*
and *u*. The old people at Philadelphia who said
"cl*a*rk" also said "m*a*rchant." And quite rightly,
for they had on their side both older English usage
and, in this case, the French spelling itself. The
sound "m*u*rchant" has come in, both in England
and in America, by exactly the same process as that by
which the sound "cl*u*rk" has come in in America,
but not in England. In these cases the words are
of Latin origin ; so is "German," which people used
to sound "Jarman"—as in the memorable story of
the Oxford University preacher who wished the
"Jarman theology" at the bottom of the "Jarman
Ocean." So with a word which easily connects itself with "clerk." The Latin "p*e*rsona" became
natural English "p*a*rson," while the more philosophical form "p*e*rson," in its many and strange
uses, is sounded as the Americans sound "clerk."
Yet I have always had a feeling for the Irish girl
who, asking in a draper's shop for "any article that
would *shoot* a young p*a*rson," was unkindly referred
to a gunmaker. But the difficulty is by no means

confined to words which we have borrowed from
Latin. Exactly the same thing happens to a crowd
of Teutonic proper names, as Derby, Berkeley,
Berkshire, Bernard, Bertram, and others. In these
names the original Old-English vowel is "*eo*;" the
modern spelling and the different modern pronun-
ciations are mere approximations, just as when the
vowel is the French or Latin *e*. One has heard
"D*a*rby" and "D*u*rby," "B*a*rkeley" and "B*u*rkeley;" and though the *a* sound is now deemed the
more polite, yet I believe that fashion has fluctuated
in this matter, as in most others. And fashion,
whether fluctuating or not, is at least inconsistent ;
if it is polite to talk of "B*a*rkshire" and "D*a*rby,"
it is no longer polite to talk about "J*a*rman" and
"J*a*rsey." But in all these cases there can be no
doubt that the *a* sound is the older. The names of
which I have spoken are often spelled with an *a* in
old writers; and the *a* sound has for it the witness
of the most familiar spelling of several of the names
when used as surnames. "Darby," "Barclay,"
"Barnard," "Bartram," all familiar surnames, show
what sound was usual when their present spelling
was fixed. Tourists, I believe, talk of the "D*u*r-
went" (as they call the Dōve the "D*u*v"); but the
Derwent at Stamfordbridge is undoubtedly "D*a*r-
went," while the more northern stream of the name

is locally "D*a*rwin," a form which has become illustrious as a surname. Now in words of this kind, while British use is somewhat fluctuating, I believe that America has universally decided for the *u* sound. But there can be no doubt that, whether in England or in America, the sound of "D*u*rby" or "B*u*rtram" is simply an attempt to adapt the sound to the spelling, while "D*a*rby" and "B*a*rtram" are the genuine traditional sounds.

Again I think I see another instance, not quite of the same kind, of the influence of the schoolmaster, in the name which in some parts of America is given to the last letter of the alphabet. This in New England is always *zee*; in the South it is *zed*, while Pennsylvania seems to halt between two opinions. Now *zed* is a very strange name. Has it anything to do with Greek *zeta*? or does it come from the old form *izzard*, which was not quite forgotten in my childhood, and which I was delighted to find remembered in America also? (*Izzard* is said to be for "*s* hard," though surely *z* is rather *s* soft). But anyhow *zee* is clearly a schoolmaster's device to get rid of the strange-sounding *zed*, and to make *z* follow the analogy of other letters. But the analogy is wrong. *Z* ought not to follow the analogy of *b*, *d*, *t*, but that of *l*, *m*, *n*, *r*, and above all of its brother *s*. If we are not to have *zed*, the name should clearly be, not *zee* but *ez*.   But it is a comfort that, besides *izzard*, I also found " ampussy and "—I hardly know how to write it—remembered beyond the Ocean, as I find that it is better known than I had thought on this side also.   " Ampussy and," that is, in full, " *and* per se, *and*," is the name of the sign for the conjunction *and*, &, which used to be printed at the end of the alphabet.   May I quote a riming nursery alphabet of my .own childhood ?   The letters have all done their several services to the apple-*pie*—not, in modern fashion, apple-*tart*—that was to be divided among them :

> Then AND came, though not one of the letters,
> And, bowing, acknowledged them all as his betters;
> And, hoping it might not be deemed a presumption,
> Remained all their honours' most humble conjunction.

The "humble conjunction" seems to have fared yet worse than Lord Macaulay's chaplain, and to have got no apple-pie at all.

Quite distinct from the pronunciation of particular words are any general characteristics in the way of utterance which speakers of English on either side may notice in speakers of English on the other side.   Americans constantly notice what they call the "English intonation," the "English accent," nay, as I have already said, the " horrible English intonation." Now I am not very clear what this accent or intonation is, and the less so as I have sometimes been told that I myself have it, sometimes that I have it not, but that I speak like an American. As no man knows exactly how he himself speaks, I cannot judge which description is the truer. On the other hand we Britishers are apt to remark in Americans something which we are tempted to call by the shorter word "twang," a description less civil perhaps than " intonation" without an adjective, but less uncivil surely than "horrible intonation." As to the origin of this "twang" I have heard various opinions. Some trace it to a theological, some to a merely geographical, cause. It has been said to be an inheritance from the Puritans as Puritans ; others say that it is simply the natural utterance of East-Anglia, without reference to sect or party. As an American mark, the thing to be most noticed about it is, that, though very common, it is far from universal. It would be in no way wonderful either if everybody spoke with a twang or if nobody spoke with a twang. But the facts, as far as I can see, are these. Some people have the twang very strongly ; some have it not at all. Some, after speaking for a long time without it, will bring it in in a particular word or sentence ; in others it is strongly marked when a few

words are uttered suddenly, but dies off in the course
of a longer conversation. And I distinctly marked
that it was far more universal among women than
among men. I could mention several American
friends from whose speech—unless possibly in particular technical words—no one could tell to which
side of the Ocean they belonged, while the utterance of their wives was distinctively American. To
us the kind of utterance of which I speak seems
specially out of place in the mouth of a graceful and
cultivated woman; but I have heard hints back
again that the speech of graceful and cultivated
Englishwomen has sometimes had just the same effect on American hearers. But, on whichever side
our taste lies, there can be little doubt that the
American utterance, be it Puritan, East-Anglian, or
anything else, is no modern innovation, but has
come by genuine tradition from the seventeenth
century.

It is otherwise with some peculiarities which concern, not the natural utterance of words to the ear,
but their artificial representation to the eye. If the
schoolmaster is a deadly foe to language, English or
any other, the printer is a foe no less deadly. Half
the unhistorical spellings which disfigure our printed
language come from the vagaries of half-learned
printers, on which side of the Ocean matters **very**

little. As for Latin words, one is sometimes tempted to say, let them spell them as they please; but it is hard when Teutonic " rime," a word which so many Romance languages have borrowed, is turned into " rhyme," merely because some printer's mind was confused between English " rime" and Greek " rhythm." So it is with specially American spelling-fancies. If any one chooses to spell words like "traveller" with one *l*, it looks odd, but it is really not worth disputing about. Nor is it worth disputing about " color" or " colour," " honor" or "honour," and the like. But when it comes to " armor," still more when it comes to " neighbor," one's Latin back in the former case, one's Teutonic back in the other, is put up. Did he who first wrote " armor" fancy that " armor" was a Latin word like " honor" or " color" ? Let *armatura*, if any one wishes it, be cut short into *armure*; but let us be spared such a false analogy as *armor*. " Arbor" for " arbour" brings out more strongly the delusion of those who, having a Latin tree on the brain, doffed Teutonic " harbour" of its aspirate. But the most unkindest cut of all is when Old-English " neáhge*búr*," which, according to the universal rule of the language, becomes in modern English "neigh*bour*," is turned into " neigh*bor*." Did anybody, even a printer or a dictionary-maker, really fancy that the last three

letters of " neighbour" had anything in common
with the last three letters of " honour"? It is surely
hardly needful to say that Old-English *ú* is in modern English consistently represented by *ou*; " hús"
becomes " house;" "súð" becomes "south;" "út"
becomes " out"—and " neáhgebúr" becomes " neigh-
bour." American printers too have some odd ways
in other matters, specially as to their way of dividing
words when part of a word has to be in one line and
part in another. Thus " nothing" will be divided,
not as " no-thing," but as " noth-ing," as if it were
the patronymic of a name " Noth." Yet surely
even a printer must have known that " nothing" is
" no-thing" and nothing else. So again " knowledge"
is divided as " knowl-edge," suggesting rather the
side of a hill than the occupation or condition of one
who knows. It is really quite possible that the *d* may
have been thrust into " knowledge"—better written
" knowlege"—from some thought of a *ledge.* Anyhow one suspects that very few people know that
ledge in " knowledge" and *lock* in " wedlock" are one
and the same ending. " Wedlock" at least is safe
from being divided as " wedl-ock" because everybody thinks that it has something to do with a lock
and key.

It would be easy to pile together a far longer

list of differences of usage in matter of speech
between England and America. But I have perhaps brought together enough to illustrate my
main general positions. I have tried to show that
so-called "Americanisms" are not to be at once
cast aside, as many people in England are inclined
to cast them aside, as if they were necessarily
corruptions of the common speech, as if it proved
something against a form of words to show that it
is usual in America, but that it is not usual in
England. Abuses of language abound in both
lands, but the conservative side of the American
character has led to the survival in America of
many good English words and phrases which have
gone out of use in England, and which ignorant
people therefore mistake for American inventions.
In other cases again, differences of usage between
the two countries are fully explained by differences
of circumstances between the two countries. In
some cases again, usages which cannot be called
correct, but which differ from mere abuses of
language, have been brought in—in either country
—through mistaken analogies or other processes
of that kind. In these different ways there has
come to be a certain distinction between the received British and the received American use of
the common English tongue, a distinction which

commonly makes it easy to see from which side of Ocean a man comes. But there is no real difference of language, not even any real difference of dialect; the speech of either side is understood without an effort by the men of the other side, and the differences are largely of a kind in which neither usage can be said to be in itself better or worse than the other.

VIII.

From language I turn, with all the diffidence of one who is not a lawyer, to say a word about law, and, with greater diffidence still, about lawyers. The lawyers in America are an even more important class than they are in England; the proportion of them in the legislative bodies both of the States and of the Union is something amazing. And the main point in which the position of the legal profession in America differs from its position in England, namely, the union of the two characters of barrister and solicitor in the same person, seems to cut two ways. On the one hand, I am told that it leads to the admission of many inferior and incompetent members of the profession, of many even who do not understand Latin. But, on the other hand, it helps, together with that localization of justice which is natural under the American system, to secure the presence of some lawyers of the higher class in every town that we come to. In England our barristers are mostly gathered together in London; in a few of the greatest towns there is a local bar; but the ordinary English town knows no resident form of lawyer higher than the local solicitor. But in America the size of the country and its Federal constitution join to hinder that centralization of the higher justice to which we are used. In all the large towns there are State courts, and often Federal courts also. And these imply the constant presence of men who answer, not to the solicitor who appears at petty sessions or in the county court, but to the barrister practising before—a layman may be forgiven for not venturing to meddle with the tribunals bearing new and longer names which have supplanted the venerable and historic courts of a few years back. Thus there is in every town a kernel of society of a higher kind than the English country-town supplies. Now in the higher class of American lawyers there is a very close tie between America and England. Where the law is simply the law of England with a difference, the old common law with such changes as later legislation may have wrought, there must be in the legal profession a good deal of knowledge of English matters. However it may be with any other class, to an educated American lawyer at least there is no need to go about to prove that America keeps the tongue and the institutions of England, not as something derived or borrowed from another people, but as the common heritage of two divided branches of the same people. To him there is no need to prove that the Englishman of America has exactly the same right in all the memories and traditions and institutions of the elder days of England that the Englishman of Britain has. For he has the surest witness of the fact constantly before his eyes. It is pleasant to see an American law library, with English and American books side by side. It is pleasant to hear an American legal pleading, in which the older English legislation, the older English decisions, are dealt with as no less binding than the legislation and decisions of the local courts and assemblies, and where the English legislation and decisions of later times are held to be, though not formally binding, yet entitled to no small respect. As to outward appearances indeed, most of the American courts have lost the pomp and circumstance with which we are accustomed to clothe the administration of the higher justice at home. It is only in that great tribunal which can sit in judgement on the legislation of a nation, in the Supreme Court of the United States, that any trace is left of the outward majesty of the law as it is understood in England. But look at any American court, in such States at least as I have visited, and we see that the real life of English law and English justice is there. All the essential principles, all the essential forms, are there. The very cry of *oyez*, meaningless most likely in the mouth of the crier who utters it, not only tells us that it is the law of England which is administering, but reminds us how largely the older law of England was recast—not more than recast—at the hands of the Norman and the Angevin. We feel that the law which is laid down by the banks of the Hudson or the Potomac is still the law of King Edward with the amendments of King William. Sometimes indeed, when we find the newer England cleaving to cumbrous traditions which the elder England has cast away, we feel that a few further amendments of later days would not be out of place. The wonderful repetitions and contradictions in the indictment against Guiteau belong to a past stage of our own jurisprudence; yet there is a certain, perhaps unreasonable, satisfaction in finding that the newer home of our people is conservative enough to cleave to some things which the elder home has exchanged for newer devices. New devices indeed we sometimes light upon in the

new world. When we look at a Maryland judge
who is authorized—with the consent to be sure of
those chiefly concerned—to send men to the gallows
without a jury, we are divided between wonder at
the innovation and awe towards a being who can do
what no other being that we ever saw before can
do. We are struck with a different feeling when
we see the mutual reverence which judge and jury
show to one another in Massachusetts, where the
judge stands up to give his charge to the jury and
the jury stand up to listen to his charge. Even
varieties of this kind, even what we are inclined to
look on as the lack of some useful solemnities, bring
more forcibly home to us that the law which is
dealt out is, after all, our own law. In this, as in
most other American matters, we notice the slightest diversity all the more because the two things
are in their main essence so thoroughly the same.

I am not forgetful that the laws of different
States are very far from being everywhere the
same, and that the legislation of some States has
brought in some startling differences from the legislation both of England and of other States. But
we may still carry on our eleventh-century formula.
The law is not a new law; it is the old law, with
certain—perhaps very considerable—amendments.
Even if it be held that a new superstructure has

been built up, it has been built up upon an old groundwork. Here there is a tie, not only to the mother-country, but to an old side of the mother-country. A real American lawyer must be an English lawyer too. He cannot fail to know something of the history of the land whose laws it becomes his duty to master; he may know at least as much as the English lawyer himself thinks it his business to know. If a good many on both sides are still floundering in the quagmire of Blackstone, there are some on both sides who have made their way to the firm ground of Stubbs and Maine.

I spoke of the indictment against Guiteau. I heard part of his trial, and a strange scene it was. From all that I saw and heard and read on the matter, I was led to the conclusion that, though some other judges on both sides of the Ocean might, simply as being stronger men, have managed the trial better, yet that the judge who tried it was not technically to blame. I gathered that he really had no power to stop Guiteau's interruptions. The constitution provides only that the prisoner shall have the "assistance of counsel." Now English counsel, and American counsel too of the higher class, would have thrown up their briefs when the prisoner insisted on talking for himself. But Guiteau's counsel were not of the higher class; and—I

speak, as a layman, with trembling—it may be
doubted whether the English usage depends on
anything more than an honourable understanding.
The truth seems to be that no lawgiver in any time
or place ever foresaw the possibility of such a prisoner as Guiteau, and that therefore there was no
law ready made which exactly suited his case.
Again, though the proceedings in the American
courts are, in all essential points—for wigs and
gowns are not essential points—so like our own,
yet the arrangements for the distribution of judicial
action are very different. In England such a case
would have been tried before a judge—perhaps
more than one judge—of the highest class. And
till I reached Washington, I took for granted that
the judge to whom so important a duty was intrusted was one of the sages of the Supreme Court.
I soon found however that Guiteau was being tried
before a magistrate of greatly inferior rank, answering rather to a recorder or a county court
judge among ourselves. The indictment, it may
be remarked, did not specify the murder of a
President as differing at all from the murder of
another man. The slain man was simply "one
James Abram Garfield, being in the peace of God
and of the United States." From the pleadings
of Guiteau's counsel I carried away one of the

choicest fallacies that I ever heard. The prisoner
must be mad, because he had shot a President
of the United States. Sane people might kill an
European king, for European kings were not the
choice of their people, and were often their oppres-
sors. But no sane man could wish to harm a President of the United States, the choice of the people.
The advocate must have underrated the intelligence
even of the black member of the jury, who must
surely have remembered that the liberator of his
race died by the hands of a murderer whom no one
looked on as mad. And it would be strange if no
one of the twelve could go on to argue that a
hereditary king, who comes to his crown by no
fault, indeed by no act, of his own, need not offend
any one by the mere fact of his accession, while the
accession of an elective magistrate must disappoint
somebody and commonly offends a powerful party.

I was unluckily able to learn next to nothing on
one of the points on which I was most anxious to
learn something. This was the administration of
justice and the general management of public business in the rural districts. My only chance was
during a sojourn in a rural part of Virginia, where,
as far as I could see, nothing of any public interest
went on at all. I did indeed see in the papers that
a judge showed himself at certain intervals in the

court-house of the county; but I had no chance of getting there. I learned indeed one thing, that the word "county" is heard at least a hundred times in Virginia, for once that it is heard in New England. This comes of the higher local organization of New England. There the township rules everything; the county is at most an aggregate of townships which has no great practical importance. In Virginia the township hardly exists; the county is the division which comes home to men in every relation of life, even more, I should say, than it does in England. On the whole, the part of Virginia that I saw rather reminded me of those ancient inhabitants of Laish who dwelled careless, quiet, and secure, who had no business with any man, and who had no magistrate to put them to shame in anything. I did not see that they wanted much putting to shame; but there seemed nobody to do it if by any chance such a course had been needed. In the towns, on the other hand, the administrators of the smaller justice are far from keeping themselves out of sight. One who has the good or bad luck to be one of the Great Unpaid in his own land is a little shocked at seeing the words "Justice of the Peace" written up over a small office. And not only are those words to be seen over a small office, they may be seen over two small offices on opposite sides of

the street, as if His Worship on either side wished
to hinder any business from going to the shop over
the way. We must allow something for the American developement of advertising; those who adver-
tise on rocks and rails will certainly not shrink from
advertising on sign-boards. Some American lawyers announce their name and calling over their
offices in a style which I fancy that no English solicitor would follow. But to the British mind there is
something strange in the notion of a Justice of the
Peace advertising his functions in the most modest
shape. Here comes in the difference between paid
and unpaid; also, I suspect, the difference between
payment by salary and payment by fees. It is directly to the advantage of the American Justice
that business should come to his office and not to
the office of the other Justice over the way.

In short, the American Justice of the Peace
holds a position quite different from, and very inferior to, the position of his English brother. So
does the American Sheriff. But I suspect that the
offices themselves in the two countries do not differ
nearly so much as the men who hold them. I mean
when the English Justice acts strictly as a Justice.
The difference shows itself in this way. The direct judicial functions of an English magistrate sitting in petty sessions are not very exalted or very

inviting. The office keeps up its position because it is unpaid, and because it carries with it a good deal of authority and local dignity in other ways. Pay the magistrate, take away his position as one of the ruling assembly of the county, leave him simply a local judge in the smallest matters, and he would most likely sink to the level of his American brother. The same kind of union of petty and sometimes disagreeable duties with power and dignity in other ways comes out still more conspicuously in the office of proctor in the English Universities. In both cases the argument is that it is well to have the inferior class of duties done by men of a higher stamp than those to whom they would be likely to fall if they stood alone. The petty police of the University can hardly be in itself attractive to a man of high scholarship and refinement. But when it is joined to a commanding position in other ways, to a kind of *tribunicia potestas*, the best men in the Universities are ready to undertake it.

The Americans are surely, on the whole, a law-abiding people. Some of them profess, and I am inclined to believe that the profession is to some extent true, that they are more than a law-abiding people, that they are a patient people. They tell us that they put up with grievances, sometimes from the law, sometimes from breakers of the law, with more of endurance than we who have stayed on this side of Ocean. On the other hand, one sometimes hears in America of breaches of the law of a peculiar kind which certainly have nothing like them in this country. I do not mean ordinary crimes, however great. I do not mean mere outbreaks of popular indignation against particular persons. The American papers, while I was in the country, contained a good many ugly stories in these ways; but I dare say it would have been easy to cap each of them by stories of the same kind in England, or at any rate elsewhere in Europe. I mean outrages directly committed against the law itself. I read an account how, not in any wild place in the far West, but in so respectable a State as Ohio, a man committed for trial, on a charge of murder, but not yet tried, was taken out of prison by a mob and hanged. And this case did not stand alone. I heard of other cases of prisons being in this way forced, and even of officers of justice being killed in resisting this specially lawless form of violence. I heard also of " Garfield avengers," people who were seeking to kill Guiteau, instead of leaving him to the slower action of the law. One such attempt was actually made, and that by one of the soldiers who were keeping guard over him. The culprit was tried by a court-martial, and, naturally and righteously, he received a heavy sentence, a long term of imprisonment. Strange to say, the man who had so directly flown in the face of the law, who had so foully betrayed his own personal trust, became an object of sympathy. He was a patriot; his patriotism took perhaps a somewhat irregular shape, but he was on the whole more to be praised than blamed. He was likened to the man who had killed the murderer of Lincoln. No analogy could be more wide of the mark. Perhaps even the killing of Booth was a little hasty; still it was done under circumstances which on the whole justified it. Booth was escaping from justice; Guiteau was safe in the hands of justice, and it was one of the officers of justice who trampled justice under foot. Yet the President was besieged by petitions for the pardon of Sergeant Mason. The feeling was not universal; wise men protested; but it was very general. I should fancy that in England any feeling of the kind would not have gone beyond that silly and, we may trust, small class which finds an object of sympathy in every criminal.

Now what is the cause of this particular form of lawlessness? I should be loath to believe that law and government which spring direct from the people are in themselves necessarily weaker than law and government which in some sort spring from a source beyond the people. I should be loath to believe that justice exercised in the name of a commonwealth has of itself less strength than justice exercised in the name of a king. It is possible that men may fancy that, by taking the law into their own hands, they are asserting their rights as the original source of the law. No notion can be more foreign to the true spirit of democracy. The source of law, the source of all authority, is the people; but the people does not mean A, B, and C, acting according to their personal pleasure; it means the whole body acting constitutionally in their assembly, primary or representative. I have always admired the usual form for the acts of a State Legislature; "The people of State A, represented by their Senate and House of Assembly, ordain as follows." But when the people have ordained, surely each one among the people has only to obey. The true democratic feeling surely is that each man in obeying the law which he has helped to make, in honouring the magistrate whom he has helped to choose, is really honouring himself and the community of which he is a part. But it is possible that there may be some minds in republican countries which cannot rise to this standard. just as

there are minds in monarchic countries which cannot understand the existence of such a standard.   It
is a fact that, at the time of the American civil
war, there were people in England who could not
understand that there could be treason or rebellion
in a republic.   I do not mean people who took up
any intelligible ground to prove that secession was
not treason or rebellion; I mean people who seriously held that, because the United States had no king,
there could not in any case be such a thing as treason or rebellion in the United States.   Still less
could the same class of people be made to understand, ten years earlier, that there could be treason
or rebellion on the part of the chosen magistrate of
a commonwealth who used the powers of his office
to overthrow that commonwealth.   Yet the mob
that breaks into a prison, that kills the gaoler or the
sheriff, and hangs the yet uncondemned prisoner,
foul as is the breach of justice and the insult to law,
does in a wild way carry out some of the objects of
law.   Those who so act are after all less guilty than
the man who upsets all law purely for own personal
ends.

It is hardly needful to attribute this kind of outrage to any necessary weakness of the law in a
democratic state.   Still it is not unlikely to be
connected with a certain weakness in the adminis-

tration of the law. If many European countries are over-governed, one may say that the United States are under-governed. It is the better fault of the two; but it surely is a fault. In the newly settled States and Territories it often happens that irregularities cannot be avoided; the law very often can be enforced only by agencies unknown to the law. There are times and places in young and rude societies where it is impossible sometimes to avoid the appeal to Mr. Justice Lynch. And even in thoroughly settled and civilized States the machinery for executing the law is often weak. The police is often insufficient; it is less uncommon than it is here for a man to find himself in that kind of case where a man must help himself or his neighbours without the countenance of any officer of the law. There is indeed a wide gap between taking the law into one's own hands when the law fails to give help, and deliberately flying in the face of the law when the law is strong enough to do its own work. Yet this last crime is more likely to come into men's heads where action, which, even if justifiable, is formally irregular, is familiar to men's minds. I thought I saw that, on the whole, human life is less thought of in America than it is in England. The fact that duels still go on is one instance out of several. The general condition of the country has a good deal to do with this state of things. Even in the old States there are large tracts which are very thinly inhabited and which cannot be called fully settled. In American travelling one is sometimes tempted to think that the only choice lies between the city and the wilderness. As we go out of New York, we soon find ourselves in a state of things far more primitive than we find at the same distance from a great English city. Wherever there is any failure in the police of the city, for that there can be no excuse; but the police of the wilderness is a thing hard to carry out under any form of government.

The action of the government again, when it does act, sometimes takes forms which are a little startling, whether in fact or in name. I came to America almost directly from lands where insurrections and civil wars are not unfrequent. I left behind me the valiant men of Crivoscia gathering on their mountains to defend the chartered rights of their fathers against the base faithlessness of their Austrian oppressor. But I did not expect to hear of insurrections and civil wars within the great republic of the West. Yet, in the course of my American sojourn, the Governor of New York found it needful to proclaim a district of his State as being in a "state of insurrection." Its inhabi-

tants had refused payment of a tax which, as far as
I could make out, had been quite lawfully voted,
but which the people of this particular place
thought to press unfairly upon them. I did not
hear how the matter ended; if it grew very serious,
it might call for the intervention of the militia of
the State, or even of the United States army. But
the "insurrection" seemed to be treated in the
newspapers as more of a joke than anything else.
So was another incident which might almost pass
for a civil war. Some Maryland fishermen had
been seeking their prey—oysters, I think it was—
in an irregular manner on the coast of Virginia.
Some said that a constable or two would have been
quite enough to assert the rights of the State and its
citizens. The Governor of Virginia, however,
thought otherwise; he forthwith gathered a fleet—
not quite, I fancy, on the scale of King Philip's ar-
mada—and went forth in person to scatter the intruders. Such an incident as this was not without
charms for a special student of federal government.

IX.

I often asked my American friends of both political parties what was the difference between them.
I told them that I could see none; both sides
seemed to me to say exactly the same things. I

sometimes got the convenient, but not wholly satis-isfactory, answer: Yes; but then we mean what we say, while the other party only pretends. Cer-tainly, when I was there, the difference between different sections of the Republican party was much clearer to an outsider than the difference between Republicans and Democrats. I found it easier to grasp the difference between a Stalwart Republican and a Republican who was not Stalwart, than to grasp the immediate difference between a Republi-can and a Democrat. On intelligible questions like Free Trade and Civil Service Reform, or again the local Virginian question of paying or not paying one's lawful debts, the division did not follow the regular cleavage of parties. Questions of this kind are plain enough; the distinction between the two great acknowledged parties is just now much less plain. So it seemed to me when I wrote in the summer of 1882, immediately after my return from America, and the elections which took place in the winter of the same year seem to bear out my con-clusion. The late Democratic victories are hardly victories over the Republican party as a party. They are more truly victories over a section of the Republican party which is eschewed by a large body of Republicans. It is hardly possible that the Democratic success can have been gained without

the help of Republican votes. But because men of
the two parties seem to say much the same things,
because they can sometimes act together when
questions occur in which principle is higher than
party, it does not at all follow that there are no differences between them. There are abiding differences between them, differences which have been
important in the past, which may be important in
the future; but just now questions which would
bring out those differences are not uppermost. I
am not sure that this is a wholesome state of things.
If there must be—and there doubtless must be—
parties in a state, it is better that they should be
divided on some intelligible difference of principle,
than that political warfare should sink into a mere
question of ins and outs, of Shanavests and Caravats. But, though the distinction between Republicans and Democrats as such does look from outside very like a distinction between Shanavests and
Caravats, it is only accidentally so. Either the
questions of the present moment may establish
fresh lines of difference, or the old and abiding distinction may some day again become as real as the
distinction between Tory and Radical, Legitimist
and Republican. Should any question ever again
arise as to the respective powers of the Union and
of the States, it is easy to see which side each party

would take. It is simply because there is no such
burning question at present stirring that the two
parties seem largely to say the same things, and yet
to be as strongly divided as ever.

I may speak on this matter as one who has made
the nature of federal government an object of special study. It strikes me that, as the doctrine of
State Rights was pushed to a mischievous extreme
twenty years and more ago, so there is danger now
of the opposite doctrine being pushed to a mischievous extreme. The more I look at the American
Union, the more convinced I am that so vast a region, taking in lands whose condition differs so
widely in everything, can be kept together only by
a federal system, leaving large independent powers
in the hands of the several States. No single parliament could legislate, no single government could
administer, for Maine, Florida, and California.
Let those States be left to a great extent independent, and they may remain united on those points
on which it is well that they should remain united.
To insist on too close an union is the very way to
lead to separation. I know of no immediate reason
to fear any attempt at centralization such as might
thus lead to separation. But it does seem to be a
possible danger; it seems to me that there are tendencies at work which are more likely to lead to

that form of error than to its opposite. In discussing this matter, I must cleave to some doctrines which I know are in some quarters looked on as obsolete. I must even cleave to the phrase "Sovereign States," though I know it may offend many. For a State is sovereign which has any powers which it holds by inherent right, without control on the part of any other power, without responsibility to any other power. Now every American State has powers of this kind. The original thirteen States did not receive their existing powers from the Union; they surrendered to the Union certain powers which were naturally their own, and kept certain others to themselves. And the later States were admitted on the same terms and to the same rights as the original thirteen. There is therefore a range within which the State is sovereign: within another range, within the range of the powers which have been surrendered to the Union, the Union is sovereign. But if it is plain matter of history that whatever powers the Union holds, it holds by the grant of the States, it is equally plain that the grant was irrevocable, except so far as its terms may be modified by a constitutional amendment. And the power of making a constitutional amendment is itself part of the grant of the States, which thus agreed that, in certain cases, a fixed majority of the States should bind the whole. The error of the Secessionists lay in treating an irrevocable grant as if it had been a revocable one. The doctrine of the right of Secession, as a constitutional right, was absurd on the face of it. Secession from the Union was as much rebellion, as much a breach of the law in force at the time, as was the original revolt of the colonies against the King. The only question in either case was whether those special circumstances had arisen which alone can justify breach of the ordinary law. But it is a pity, in avoiding this error, to run into the opposite one, and to hold, not only that the grant made by the States to the Union was irrevocable, but that the grant was really made the other way. I find that it is the received doctrine in some quarters that the States have no rights but such as the Union allows to them. One of the Boston newspapers was angry because I put forth in one of my lectures the plain historical fact that the States, as, in theory at least, independent commonwealths, surrendered certain defined powers to the Union, and kept all other powers in their own hands. The Boston paper was yet more angry because a large part of a Boston audience warmly cheered—warmly, that is, for Boston—such dangerous doctrines. I was simply ignorant; those who cheered me were something worse.

Now notions of this kind are not confined to a single newspaper. And they surely may lead to results as dangerous at one end as the doctrine of Secession was at the other. Both alike cut directly at the very nature of a federal system. Connected perhaps with this tendency is one of those changes in ordinary speech which come in imperceptibly, without people in general remarking them, but which always prove a great deal. In England we now universally use the word " Government" where in my boyhood everybody said " Ministry" or " Ministers." Then it was " the Duke of Wellington's *Ministry* " or Lord Grey's; now it is " Lord Beaconsfield's *Government* " or Mr. Gladstone's. This change, if one comes to think about it, certainly means a great deal.* So it means a great deal that, where the word " federal " used to be used up to the time of the civil war or later, the word " national " is now used all but invariably. It used to be " federal capital," " federal army," " federal revenue," and so forth. Now the word " national " is almost always used instead. I have now and then seen the word " federal " used in the

---

* I find that I made this remark as long ago as 1864. See " Historical Essays," First Series, p. 384 (Presidential Government).

old way, but so rarely that I suspect that it was
used of set purpose, as a kind of protest, as I might
use it myself. Now there is not the slightest objec-
tion to the word "national;" for the union of the
States undoubtedly forms, for all political purposes,
a nation. The point to notice is, not the mere use
of the word "national," but the displacement of the
word "federal" in its favour. This surely marks a
tendency to forget the federal character of the
national government, or at least to forget that its
federal character is its very essence. The difference
between a federal government and one not federal
is a difference of original structure which runs
through everything. It is a far wider difference
than the difference between a kingdom and a republic, which may differ only in the form given to the
executive. It is perfectly natural that the word
"federal" should be in constant use in a federal
state, in far more common use than any word im-
plying kingship need be in a kingdom. There is a
constant need to distinguish things which come
within the range of the federal power from things
which come within the range of the State or canton.
And for this purpose the word "federal" is more
natural than the word "national." The proper
range of the latter word surely lies in matters which
have to do with other nations. One would speak of

the national honour, but of the federal revenue. That " national " should have driven out "federal " within a range where the latter word seems so specially at home does really look as if the federal character of the national power was, to say the least, less strongly present to men's minds than it was twenty years back.

The historical connexion between the written constitution of the United States and the unwritten constitution of England is a truth on which I have often tried to insist, and not least when I was lecturing on such matters in the United States themselves. I will not here go into the subject at length; it may be enough to speak of the most remarkable case of the closeness with which the daughter has, wherever it has been possible, reproduced the parent. This is the prevalence of legislative bodies composed of two houses, a system which may be studied alike in the Union, in the States, and in many at least of the cities. We are so familiar with the system of two Houses, from its reproduction in countless later constitutions, that we are apt to forget that, when the federal constitution of the United States was drawn up, that system was by no means the rule, and that its adoption in the constitution of the United States was a remarkable instance of cleaving to the institutions of the mother-country. Though the United States Senate, the representative of the separate being and political equality of the States, has some functions quite different from those of the House of Lords, yet it could hardly have come into the heads of constitution-makers who were not familiar with the House of Lords. I may here quote the remark of an acute American friend that the Senate is as much superior to the House of Lords as the House of Representatives is inferior to the House of Commons. A neat epigram of this kind is seldom literally true; but this one undoubtedly has truth in it. It follows almost necessarily from the difference between the British and American constitutions that the Upper House of the American Congress should be in character and public estimation really the Upper House. In Great Britain no statesman of the first rank and in the vigour of life has any temptation to exchange the House of Commons for the House of Lords. By so doing he would leave an assembly of far greater practical authority for one of much less. But in the United States such a statesman has every temptation to leave the House of Representatives for the Senate as soon as he can. As neither House can directly overthrow a Government in the way that the House of Commons can in England, while the Senate has a share in various acts of the Executive

power with which the House of Representatives
has nothing to do, the Senate is clearly the assembly
of greater authority. Its members, chosen for six
years by the State Legislatures, while the Representatives are chosen by the people for two years,
have every advantage as to the tenure of their seats,
and it is not wonderful to find that re-election is far
more the rule in the Senate than in the House. I
had to explain more than once that it was a rare
thing in England for a member of Parliament to
lose his seat, unless he had given some offence to his
own party, or unless the other party had grown
strong enough to bring in a man of its own. In
America, it seems, it is not uncommon for a Representative to be dismissed by his constituents of his
own party, simply because it is thought that he has
sat long enough, and because another man would
like the place. Here the difference between paid
and unpaid members comes in : where members are
paid, there will naturally be a larger stock of eager
candidates to choose from. I was present at sittings
of both Houses, and there was certainly a most
marked difference in point of order and decorum
between the two. The Senate seemed truly a Senate; the House of Representatives struck me as
a scene of mere hubbub rather than of real debate.
One incident specially struck me as illustrating the

constitutional provision which shuts out the Ministers of the President from Congress. One Representative made a fierce attack on the Secretary of the
Navy, and the Secretary of the Navy was not there
to defend himself. Generally I should say, the
House of Representatives and the Legislative bodies
which answer to it in the several States illustrate
Lord Macaulay's saying about the necessity of a
Ministry to keep a Parliament in order. One result of its absence is the far larger powers which in
these assemblies are given to the Speaker. And
this is again attended by the danger of turning the
Speaker himself into the instrument of a party.

The differences of procedure between our Houses
of Parliament and the American assemblies, both of
the Union and of the States, are very curious and
interesting, specially just now when the question of
Parliamentary procedure has taken to itself so much
attention. But I must go on to give my impressions
of other matters, rather than attempt to enlarge on
a point which I cannot say that I have specially
studied. The State legislatures are the features of
American political life which are most distinctive
of the federal system, and to which there cannot be
anything exactly answering among ourselves. It
must always be remembered that a State legislature
does not answer to a town council or a court of

quarter sessions. It is essentially a parliament, though a parliament with limited functions, and which can never be called on to deal with the highest questions of all. The range of the State legislatures is positively very wide, and takes in most things which concern the daily affairs of mankind. But a large part of their business commonly consists in the passing of private bills, acts of incorporation, and the like. Some States seem to have found that constant legislation on such matters was not needed, and have therefore thought good that their legislatures should meet only every other year. In Pennsylvania, therefore, where I had good opportunities of studying some other matters, I had no opportunity of studying the working of a State legislature. When I was there, municipal life was in full vigour in Philadelphia, but State life was dead at Harrisburg. But I came in for a sight of the legislature of New York at the time of the "dead lock" early in 1882. For week after week the Lower House found it impossible to elect a Speaker. And this was not the result of absolute equality between the two great parties. It was because a very small body of men, who had no chance of carrying a candidate from among themselves, thought fit, in ballot after ballot, to hinder the election of the acknowledged candidate of either side.

This illustrates the result of the rule which requires an absolute majority. I pointed out to several friends on the spot that no such dead lock could have happened in the British House of Commons, where the candidate who received most votes would have been elected, without any further reckonings. I know not how far the existence of a regular Ministry and Opposition would hinder the possibility of this particular kind of scandal; but it is hard to conceive the existence of a ministry in our sense in a State constitution. Even in our still dependent colonies, the reproduction of our system of ministries going in and out in consequence of a parliamentary vote may be thought to be somewhat out of place. Still the Governor, named by an external power, has much of the position of a king, and his relations to his ministry and his parliament can in a manner reproduce those of the sovereign in the mother-country. But it is hard to conceive an elective Governor, above all the Governor of such a State as Rhode Island or Delaware, working through the conventionalities of a responsible ministry. I would indeed go further, and say that the ministerial system is out of place in a republic of any kind and on any scale. The whole idea of the responsible ministry is that they stand in front of the irresponsible king, that his acts are done by their advice, and that they take on themselves the praise or blame of them. The king reigns, but his ministers govern. But in a republic we naturally expect that the President, Governor, or other chief magistrate, chosen, therefore chosen presumably for his personal fitness, will himself govern, within the range of such powers as the law gives him. He may need ministers as assistants in governing; he does not need them to take on themselves the responsibility of his acts. Indeed even in such a State as New York there is still something patriarchal about the office of Governor. While I was in the capitol at Albany, the friends of a condemned criminal came to plead with the Governor in person for the exercise of his prerogative of mercy. Now the population of the State of New York, swollen by one overgrown city, is greater than that of Ireland; even in its natural state, it would be much greater than that of Scotland. I thought of the days when the King did sit in the gate.

The personal heads of the Union, the State, and the City, the President, the Governor, the Mayor, all come from English tradition. If we study the commonwealths of other ages and countries, we shall see that this great position given to a single man, though by no means without precedent, is by

no means the rule. The title of Governor especially is directly handed on from the days before independence. It would hardly have suggested itself
to the founders of commonwealths which had not
been used to the Governor sent by the King. The
powers of the Governor and the duration of his
office differ widely in different States, even in
neighbouring and closely kindred States. The
Governor of Massachusetts still keeps up a good
deal of dignity, while the Governor of Connecticut
is a much smaller person. But the Governor of
Connecticut holds office for a longer time than his
brother of Massachusetts. The Mayor too does not
hold exactly the same place in every city. At
Brooklyn, when I was there, a great point in the
way of reform was held to have been won by
greatly enlarging the powers of the Mayor. Men
who can well judge hold that purity of administration is best attained by vesting large powers in
single persons, elective, responsible, acting under
the eye of the public. And I was told that, even
in the worst cases, better results come from the
election of single officers than from the election of
larger numbers. The popular election of Judges,
which has been introduced into many States, is one
of the things which British opinion would be most
united in condemning. We should all agree in

wishing that both the Federal courts and the courts
of those States which, like Massachusetts, cleave to
older modes of appointment may stay as they are.
But, from what I could hear, both in New York
and in other States which have adopted the elec-
tive-system, the results are better than might have
been expected. Each party, it is said, makes it a
point of honour to name fairly competent candidates
for the judicial office. So again, the municipal
administration of New York City was for years a
byword, and the name of Alderman was anything
but a name of honour. But, even in the worst
times, the post of Mayor was almost always respec-
tably filled. Even, so I was told, in one case where
the previous record of the elected Mayor was noto-
riously bad, his conduct in office was not to be
blamed.

The prevalence of corruption in various shapes in
various branches of the administration of the United
States is an ugly subject, on which I have no
special facts to reveal. The mere fact of corruption
cannot be fairly laid to the charge of any particular
form of government, though particular forms of
government will doubtless cause corruption to take
different shapes. It is absurd to infer that a democratic or a federal form of government has a necessary and special tendency to corruption, when it is

certain that corruption has been and is just as rife under governments of other kinds. The great source of corruption in America is doubtless the system of "spoils" in the administration of federal patronage, the system by which, on every party success in the choice of a President, a clean sweep is made, not only of the holders of high political office, who must naturally expect to be changed, but of federal office-bearers, great and small, throughout the country. Such a system is of course inconsistent with the existence of any efficient civil service; it opens the way for a vast deal of corruption in various shapes, and it sets the example for a vast deal of corruption in other branches. To me, I must confess, the feeling which it takes for granted seems somewhat strange. The love of office, in the shape which it often takes in America, is rather hard to understand. I can understand a man taking a great post, say a foreign legation or a seat in the cabinet, even with the certainty that it must be resigned at the end of four years. I do not understand any one wishing for smaller offices which carry no special dignity or authority, and which must be an interruption to a man's ordinary career, whatever that may be. I can understand a man entering the post-office or any other branch of the public service, as the work of his life; I cannot

understand a man wishing to be a local postmaster
for four years and no longer. Yet the number of
office-seekers—the word has becomingly followed
the thing—in America is very wonderful. But, as
far as I can see, this system is condemned, in theory
at least, by all except those who hope to profit by
it. Still a system in which so many are interested,
and in which so many more hope that they may be,
will, it is to be feared, prove hard to get rid of.
But I imagine that the elections of the fall of 1882
must be taken, less as a party victory of the Democratic side, than as a protest against this and other
forms of corruption. And, while I am revising
what I wrote a few months back, I see that the
question of Civil Service Reform is practically taken
up by the Federal Legislature. In this matter
the loss of Garfield will doubtless be deeply felt.
When I reached America, the immediate mourning
for the murdered President was hardly over; before I came away, the natural reaction had begun;
some newspapers had begun to speak against his
memory. Yet the general conviction seemed very
deep that the loss was a real and heavy one, and
that the great work of purifying the Federal
administration had undergone a great check. I
always heard Garfield's position in the House of
Representatives spoken of as something quite ex-

ceptional, as an instance of the direct influence of
an upright and noble personal character. The loss
to his country was great; for himself we may say
that it was well that he did not recover. Worthy
of honour as the real Garfield was, no man, not Marcus or Alfred or Saint Lewis, could have lived up
to the standard of the ideal Garfield.

In my own small experience what most struck
me was the way in which, in discussing matters of
almost every kind, corruption seemed to be taken
for granted as a matter of course. This is akin to
the curious fact that the word "politics" and "politician" should have put on a meaning which, if not
positively discreditable, has a tendency that way.
Among ourselves I do not think that the word
"politics" has at all a bad sense; but the word
"politician" is now seldom used, and, when it was
more commonly used, as it was in my boyhood, it
had something disparaging about it. The tendency
I mean, that of assuming corruption where one
would not have thought that the idea could have
come in, is one of which some instances will be
more in place further on. It often came out in
discussing local matters, sometimes matters which
seemed to have nothing whatever to do with politics. This struck me specially in the State of New
York, and sometimes with reference to very small

matters indeed. As for strictly electoral corruption, it seems to take different shapes on the two
sides of Ocean. In America I heard something of
bribery of the electors, but certainly very much
less than we are used to in England. After I came
back to England, I was walking in an English city
with an American and an English friend. We
chanced to meet one of those gentlemen who were
unlucky in the early days of the present Parliament. When he was gone by, my English friend
pointed him out to the American as " the corrupt
member." The phrase was perhaps not happily
chosen; at any rate it was altogether misunderstood. When all that was meant was corruption of
the electors, the thought suggested to the American
mind was a corrupt use of his vote in Parliament,
which I need not say was not thought of for a
moment. At the elections themselves, the danger
which, at Philadelphia at least, seemed most to be
feared was not bribery, but fraudulent returns.
These, I think, are never heard of among us. I
never remember to have heard of any Mayor or
Sheriff being suspected of wilfully making other
than a true return of the votes actually given, by
whatever means those votes might have been ob-
tained. With us the returning officer and his agents
are held to be at least officially impartial; it is their

business to put their party politics in their pockets
for the time. I know not how things are done in
those parliamentary boroughs which have no cor-
porations; in an ordinary county or borough, the
Sheriff or Mayor has the advantage of not being
appointed with any direct reference to the election;
he is appointed for other purposes also, and an
election may or may not happen during his term
of office. But when election-inspectors are elected
on the general electoral ticket, that is, when the
official person represents the party dominant in the
place, it is clear that the temptations to unfairness
are greatly increased.

I was greatly interested in the municipal election
which I saw at Philadelphia early in 1882. The
municipal administration of that city has, like that
of New York, long had a bad name. Corruption,
jobbery, the rule of rings and " bosses," and above
all, what to us sounds odd, the corrupt administration of the Gas Trust, were loudly complained of.
And I certainly am greatly deceived if what I saw
and studied was anything but a vigorous and
honest effort to bring in a better state of things.
Republicans and Democrats brought themselves to
forget their party differences, or rather party
names, and to work together for the welfare and
honour of their common city. The movement was

described to me, in a way at which I have already
hinted, as an union of the honest men of both parties against the rogues of both parties. And such,
as far as I could judge, it really was. I did indeed
hear it whispered that such fits of virtue were
not uncommon, both in Philadelphia and elsewhere,
that they wrought some small measure of reform for
a year or two, but that, in order to keep the ground
that had been gained, a continuous effort was
needed which men were not willing to make, and
that things fell back into their old corrupt state.
And it is plain that the man who gains by main-
taining corruption is likely to make great habitual
efforts to keep up a corrupt system, while the man
who opposes it, who gains nothing by opposing it,
but who gives up his time, his quiet, and his ordinary business, for the public good, is tempted at
every moment to relax in his efforts. This failure
of continued energy is just what Dêmosthenês
complains of in the Athenians of his day; and experience does seem to show that here is a weak side
of democratic government. To keep up under a
popular system an administration at once pure and
vigorous does call for constant efforts on the part of
each citizen which it needs some self-sacrifice to
make. The old saying that what is everybody's
business is nobody's business becomes true as re-

gards the sounder part of the community. But it follows next that what is everybody's business becomes specially the business of those whose business one would least wish it to be. Yet my Philadelphian friends assured me that they had been steadily at work for ten years, that they had made some way every year, but that last year they had made more way than they had ever made before. The immediate business was to dislodge " bosses" and other corrupt persons from the municipal councils, and to put in their stead men of character and ability, whether Republican or Democratic in politics. And this object, surely one much to be sought for, was, as far as I could see, largely carried out. I did indeed hear the murmurs of one or two stern Republicans, who could not bring themselves to support a list which contained any Democratic names. But the other view seemed to be the popular one. I read much of the fugitive election literature, and attended one of the chief ward-meetings. I was greatly struck by the general hearty enthusiasm in what was not a party struggle, but an honest effort for something above party. The speaking was vigorous, straightforward, often in its way eloquent. It was somewhat more personal than we are used to in England, even at an election. But here again the comparison is perhaps not a fair one. As

I before said, I know nothing of English municipal elections, and the Philadelphian reformers had to deal with evils which have no parallel in the broader walks of English political life. Whatever may be our side in politics, we have no reason to suspect our opponents of directly filling their pockets at the public cost.

A municipal election is of more importance in America than it is in England, because of the large powers, amounting to powers of local legislation, which are vested in the cities. This would seem to be the natural tendency of a Federal system. It would indeed be inaccurate to say that the City is to the State what the State is to the Union. For the powers of the city may of course be modified by an act of the State Legislature, just as the powers of an English municipal corporation may be modified by an Act of Parliament, while no mere act of Congress, nothing short of a constitutional amendment, can touch the powers of a sovereign State. But it is natural for a member of an Union, keeping independent powers by right, to allow to the members of its own body a large amount of local independence, held not of right but of grant. It strikes us as strange that, owing to the American electoral arrangements, no man can stand up in Congress and say " I am member for New York or

Boston or Philadelphia;" but, as to its own local
affairs, an American city is more thoroughly a commonwealth, it has more of the feelings of a commonwealth, than an English city has. As for the
use of the name, we must remember that in the
United States every corporate town is called a
"city," while, in some States at least, what we
should call a market-town bears the legal style of
"village." In New England the cities are inter-
lopers. They have largely obscured the older constitution of the *towns*. The word *town* in New
England does not, as with us, mean a collection of
houses, perhaps forming a political community, perhaps not. It means a certain space on the earth's
surface, which may or may not contain a town in
our sense, but whose inhabitants form a political
community in either case. Its assembly is the town-
meeting, the survival, or rather revival, of the old
Teutonic assembly on the soil of the third England.
This primitive institution best keeps its ancient
character in the country districts and among the
smaller towns in our sense of the word. Where a
"city" has been incorporated, the ancient constitution has lost much of its importance. It has not
been abolished. In some cases at least the two constitutions, of town and city, the Teutonic primary
assembly and the later system of representative

bodies, go on side by side in the same place. Each has its own range of subjects; but it is the tendency of the newer institution to overshadow the older. I deeply regret that I left America without seeing a New England town-meeting with my own eyes. It was a thing which I had specially wished to see, if only in order to compare it with what I had seen in past years in Uri and Appenzell. But when I was first in New England, it was the wrong time of the year, and my second visit was very short. I thus unavoidably lost a very favourable chance of seeing what I conceive that the English parish vestry ought to be but is not. And I am not sure that some of my New England friends did not look a little black at me, because the immediate cause of my failure was an old-standing engagement to a gentleman of New York of Democratic principles.

When engaged in comparing the constitutions of England and of the United States, I have sometimes gone so far as to think that it might be a good test of those who have and those who have not made a scientific study of comparative politics, to see whether they are most struck by the likenesses or by the unlikenesses of the two systems. The close analogy in the apportionment of power among the elements of the State, the general relations of

President, Senate, and House of Representatives, are points of likeness of far more moment even than the difference in the form of the Executive, much more so than the different constitution of the Upper House. The differences are indeed many and important; the trial is to see the real likeness through the differences. The American constitution in short, as I have rather made it my business to preach, is the English constitution with such changes—very great and important changes beyond doubt—as change of circumstances made needful. But as those circumstances have certainly not been changed back again, it is at least not likely that the constitution of America will ever be brought nearer than it now is to the constitution of England, however likely it may be that the constitution of England may some day be brought nearer to the constitution of America. It was therefore with unfeigned wonder that I read the reflexions of an English member of Parliament who lately gave the world his impressions of American travel. He, too, was struck with the likeness between the two systems; but the practical inference which he drew from the likeness was that the American system might easily be brought into complete conformity with the English model. The President was so like a King that it would be easy to change him into one; the Senate was so like a House of Lords that it would be easy to change it into one. It only needed to bring the hereditary principle into both institutions, and the thing would be done at once. Yes; only how could the hereditary principle be brought in? Where are the hereditary king and the hereditary lords to be found? This ingenious political projector forgot that you cannot call hereditary kings and hereditary lords into being by a constitutional amendment. If one could ever be tempted to use the ugly and outlandish word *prestige*, it would be to explain the position held by such hereditary elements in a free state. Where they exist, they certainly have a kind of effect on the mind which can hardly be accounted for by any rational principle, and which does savour of something like sleight-of-hand. Where they exist, their existence is the best argument in their favour, and by virtue of that argument they may go on existing for ages. But you cannot create them at will. A deep truth was uttered by the genealogist who lamented the hard fate of Adam in that he could not possibly employ himself with his own favourite study. And in no time or place would an attempt at creating hereditary offices of any kind seem to be more hopeless than in the United States at the present day. Genealogy is a favourite American study; but it is not studied with any political object. The destiny of the country has gone steadily against the growth of any hereditary traditions. There has been no opportunity, such as there often has been in other commonwealths, for the growth of an ascendency in particular families which might form the kernel of an aristocratic body. The first President and nearly all his most eminent successors left no direct male descendants or no descendants at all. It is only in the family of the second President that anything like hereditary eminence has shown itself, and the two Adamses were the two among the earlier and greater Presidents who failed to obtain re-election. Since their days everything has tended more and more in the opposite direction; every year that the Union has lasted has made such dreams as those of our English legislator more and more utterly vain. When a thing is said to lie "beyond the range of practical politics," it commonly means that it will become the most immediately practical of all questions a few months hence. But one might really use the phrase in safety when dealing with such a scheme as that of changing the elective President into a hereditary King and the elective Senate into a hereditary House of Lords.

X.

My contention throughout my whole argument is that the great land of which I am speaking is still essentially an English land. It is no small witness to the toughness of fibre in the English folk wherever it settles that it is so. A land must be reckoned as English where a great majority of the people must still be of English descent, where the speech is still the speech of England, where valuable contributions are constantly made to English literature, where the law is still essentially the law of England, and where valuable contributions are constantly made to English jurisprudence. A land must be reckoned as English where the English kernel is so strong as to draw to itself every foreign element, where the foreign settler is adopted into the English home of an English people, where he or his children exchange the speech of their elder dwellings for the English speech of the land. Men of various nationalities are, on American ground, easily changed into " good Americans," and the " good American" must be, in every sense that is not strictly geographical or political, a good Englishman. And, as regards a large part of the foreign settlers, no man of real English feeling can wish to give them other than a hearty welcome.

The German, and still more the Scandinavian, settlers are simply men of our own race who have
lagged behind in the western march, but who have
at last made it at a single pull, without tarrying for
a thousand years in the isle of Britain. But there
are other settlers, other inmates, with whose presence
the land, one would think, might be happy to dis-
pense. I must here speak my own mind, at the
great risk of offending people on more sides than
one. Men better versed in American matters than
myself point out to me the fact that the negro vote
balances the Irish vote. But one may be allowed
to think that an Aryan land might do better still
without any negro vote, that a Teutonic land might
do better still without any Irish vote. And what
I venture to say on the housetops has been whispered in my ear in closets by not a few in America
who fully understand the state and the needs of
their country. Very many approved when I suggested that the best remedy for whatever was amiss
would be if every Irishman should kill a negro and
be hanged for it. Those who dissented dissented
most commonly on the ground that, if there were
no Irish and no negroes, they would not be able to
get any domestic servants. The most serious objec-
tion came from Rhode Island, where they have no
capital punishment, and where they had no wish to

keep the Irish at the public expense. Let no one think that I have any ill-feeling towards the Irish people. In their own island I have every sympathy with them. More than eight years back I argued in the pages of the "Fortnightly Review" on behalf of Home Rule, or of any form of Irish independence which did not involve, as some schemes then proposed did involve, the dependence of Great Britain. I should indeed be inconsistent if I were to refuse to the Irishman what I have sought to win for the Greek, the Bulgarian, and the Dalmatian. Nor is it wonderful or blameworthy if men who have left their old homes to escape from the wrongs of foreign rule should carry with them into their new homes the memory of the wrongs which drove them from the old. I share a natural indignation against those who, either in Ireland or in America, make a good cause to be evil spoken of; but, as long as the Irishman seeks to compass his ends only by honourable means, we have no right to blame him merely because his ends are different from ours. But all this is perfectly consistent with the manifest fact that the Irish element is, in the English lands on both sides of the Ocean, a mischievous element. The greatest object of all is for the severed branches of the English folk to live in the fullest measure of friendship and unity that is consistent with their severed state. Now the Irish element in America is the greatest of all hindrances in the way of this happy state of things. It is the worst, and perhaps the strongest, of the causes which help to give a bad name to American politics. Political men in all times and places lie under strong temptations to say and do things which they otherwise would not say and do, in order to gain some party advantage. But on no political men of any time or place has this kind of influence been more strongly brought to bear than it is on political men in the United States who wish to gain the Irish vote. The importance of that vote grows and grows; no party, no leading man, can afford to despise it. Parties and men are therefore driven into courses to which otherwise they would have no temptation to take, and those for the most part courses which are unfriendly to Great Britain. Any ill-feeling which other causes may awaken between the two severed branches of the English people is prolonged and strengthened by the presence of the Irish settlers in America. In some minds they may really plant hostile feelings towards Great Britain which would otherwise find no place there. At any rate they plant in many minds a habit of speaking and acting as if such hostile feelings did find a place, a habit which cannot but lead to bad effects in many ways.

The mere rumour, the mere thought, of recalling Mr. Lowell from his post in England in subserviency to Irish clamour is a case in point. That such a thing should even have been dreamed of, as it was last year, shows the baleful nature of Irish influence in America. It shows how specially likely it is to stir up strife and ill-feeling between Great Britain and America, even at times when, setting Irish matters aside, there is not the faintest ground of quarrel on either side. In a view of poetical justice, it is perhaps not unreasonable that English misrule in Ireland should be punished in this particular shape. It may be just that the wrongs which we have done to our neighbours should be paid off at the hands of members of our own family. But the process is certainly unpleasant to our branch of the family, and it is hard to see how it can be any real gain to the other.

But the Irishman is, after all, in a wide sense, one of ourselves. He is Aryan; he is European; he is capable of being assimilated by other branches of the European stock. There is nothing to be said against this or that Irishman all by himself. In England, in America, in any other land, nothing hinders him from becoming one with the people of the land, or from playing an useful and honourable part among them.

All that is needed to this end is that he should come all by himself. It is only when Irishmen gather in such numbers as to form an Irish community capable of concerted action that any mischief is to be looked for from them. The Irish difficulty is troublesome just now; it is likely to be troublesome for some time to come; but it is not likely to last for ever. But the negro difficulty must last, either till the way has been found out by which the Ethiopian may change his skin, or till either the white man or the black departs out of the land. The United States—and, in their measure, other parts of the American continent and islands—have to grapple with a problem such as no other people ever had to grapple with before. Other communities, from the beginning of political society, have been either avowedly or practically founded on distinctions of race. There has been, to say the least, some people or nation or tribe which has given its character to the whole body, and by which other elements have been assimilated. In the United States this part has been played, as far as the white population is concerned, by the original English kernel. Round that kernel the foreign elements have grown; it assimilates them; they do not assimilate it. But beyond that range lies another range where assimilation ceases to be possible. The eternal laws of nature, the eternal distinction of colour, forbid the assimilation of the negro. You may give him the rights of citizenship by law; you cannot make him the real equal, the real fellow, of citizens of European descent. Never before in our world, the world of Rome and of all that Rome has influenced, has such an experiment been tried. And this, though in some ages of the Roman dominion the adoption and assimilation of men of other races was carried to the extremest point that the laws of nature would allow. Long before the seat of Empire was moved to Constantinople, the name of Roman had ceased to imply even a presumption of descent from the old patricians and plebeians. A walk through any collection of Roman inscriptions will show how, in the later days of the undivided Empire, a man was far oftener succeeded by his freedman than by his son. And besides freedmen, strangers of every race within the Empire had been freely admitted to citizenship, and were allowed to bear the names of the proudest Roman *gentes*. The Julius, the Claudius, the Cornelius of those days was for the most part no Roman by lineal descent, but a Greek, a Gaul, a Spaniard, or an Illyrian. But the Gaul, the Spaniard, the Illyrian, could all be assimilated; they could all be made into Romans. They learned

to speak and act in everything as men no less truly
Roman than the descendants of the first settlers on
the Palatine. Such men ceased to be Gauls, Span-
iards, or Illyrians. The Greek, representative of a
richer and more perfect speech, of a higher and
older civilization, could become for many purposes
a Roman without ceasing to be a Greek. In all
these cases no born physical or intellectual difference parted off the slave from his master, the
stranger from the citizen. When the artificial distinction was once taken away, in the next generation at least all real distinction was lost. This cannot be when there is an eternal physical and intellectual difference between master and slave, between
citizen and stranger. The Roman Senate was
crowded with Gauls almost from the first moment
of the conquest of Gaul; but for a native Egyptian
to find his way there was a rare portent of later
times. No edict of Antoninus Caracalla could turn
him into a Roman, as the Gauls had been turned
long before that edict. The bestowal of citizenship
on the negro is one of those cases which show what
law can do and what it cannot. The law may de-
clare the negro to be the equal of the white man;
it cannot make him his equal. To the old question,
Am I not a man and a brother? I venture to
answer: No. The negro may be a man and a

brother in some secondary sense; he is not a man
and a brother in the same full sense in which every
Western Aryan is a man and a brother. He cannot
be assimilated; the laws of nature forbid it. And
it is surely a dangerous experiment to have in any
commonwealth an inferior race, legally equal to the
superior, but which nature keeps down below the
level to which law has raised it. It is less dangerous
in this particular case, because the negro is on the
whole a peaceful and easily satisfied creature. He
has no very lofty ambition; he is for the most part
contented to imitate the ways of the white man as
far as he can. A high-spirited people in the same
case would be a very dangerous element indeed.
No one now pleads for slavery; no one laments the
abolition of slavery; but did the abolition of slavery
necessarily imply the admission of the emancipated
slave to full citizenship? There is, I allow, difficulty and danger in the position of a class enjoying
civil but not political rights, placed under the pro-
tection of the law, but having no share in making
the law or in choosing its makers. But surely there
is still greater difficulty and danger in the existence
of a class of citizens who at the polling-booth are
equal to other citizens, but who are not their equals
anywhere else. We are told that education has
done and is doing much for the younger members

of the once enslaved race. But education cannot wipe out the eternal distinction that has been drawn by the hand of nature. No teaching can turn a black man into a white one. The question which, in days of controversy, the North heard with such wrath from the mouth of the South, "Would you like your daughter to marry a nigger?" lies at the root of the matter. Where the closest of human connexions is, in any lawful form, looked on as impossible, there is no real brotherhood, no real fellowship. The artificial tie of citizenship is in such cases a mockery. One has heard of negro senators and negro representatives; but their day seems to have gone by. And I cannot help thinking that those in either hemisphere who were most zealous for the emancipation of the negro must, in their heart of hearts, feel a secret shudder at the thought that, though morally impossible, it is constitutionally possible, that two years hence a black man may be chosen to sit in the seat of Washington and Garfield.

As far as my own means of observation went, though this is the kind of point on which every man does well to distrust conclusions which must necessarily be partial, it struck me that the feelings of the two parts of the country towards the negro had in some sort changed places. Before the war we always understood that the Northern people, while professing zeal for the freedom of the negroes, shrank from them personally, but that the Southern people, while anxious to keep them in bondage, felt no such personal shrinking. The feeling both ways seems perfectly natural. To me at least the negro is repulsive; but I can understand that he may be otherwise to those who have been used to him from their childhood. On the other hand, I can understand that, now that the negroes have been set free by the agency of the North against the will of the South, the one side may think it their duty to make the best that they can of their own work, while the other side may feel a very natural bitterness towards those whose freedom is a constant memorial of their defeat. I certainly heard people speak of the negro in a different tone in the two great sections of the country. In the North it struck me that people tried to speak as well of the negro as they could; in Virginia there seemed no such necessity. But nowhere has the negro made any approach to real social equality. I need hardly say that I never met a negro at any American gentleman's table. I did hear of one gentleman—I think at Washington—who had a single white man in his service, the others being negroes. But the white man, if he waited on his master, was waited on by his fellow-servants;

he dined at a table by himself, while the inferior race served him. In the North the servants are largely Irish or other strangers; in the Virginian farm-house of which I am thinking, all the servants, indoors and out, were black; what seemed strange to English notions, none of them slept in the house. And the broad distinction between the two races, as wiping out distinctions between members of the same race, sometimes leads to odd consequences. If a white workman, for instance, has to be employed for the whole day, he must dine at the master's table; he will not eat and drink with coloured people.

Still we must not forget that there are great differences among the so-called coloured people, some doubtless owing to their different fates since their forced migration, others owing to older differences in their first African homes. Several writers have pointed out that, under the general head of negroes, blacks, coloured people, we jumble together men of nations differing widely in speech, in original geographical position, in physical qualities, probably in intellectual qualities too, most certainly in different degrees of blackness. I fancy that the case is very much as if the tables had been turned, as if Africa had enslaved Europeans, and as if Greeks, Frenchmen, and Swedes had been jumbled together under the common name of Whites. And though education cannot undo the work of nature, though it cannot raise the lower race to the level of the upper, it may do much to improve the lower race within its own range. A negro in New England certainly differs a good deal from a negro in Missouri. For the negro in New England very likely comes of a free father and grandfather, and the fact of a negro being free a generation or two back was a pretty sure sign of his belonging to the more energetic class of his fellows. Such an one has lived with white men, not indeed on equal terms, but on terms which have enabled him to master their language and a good deal of their manners. But the negro in Missouri has very likely been himself a slave, perhaps a plantation slave. To the stranger at least the speech of such negroes is hard to be understood. As far as I heard it, it was not the racy dialect of Uncle Remus. It may have been my fancy, but it certainly struck my ear as the speech, not of foreigners who found it hard to speak English but who might be eloquent in some other tongue, but of beings to whom the art of speech in any shape was not altogether familiar. No doubt the real fact was that they had, as was not unlikely in their position, lost their own tongue without having fully found ours. If a small vocabulary is enough for the wants of an English labourer, one smaller still must have been enough for the wants of a plantation negro. The African languages have, I believe, altogether died out everywhere, and, from all that I could learn, the comic and joyous element of the negro character seems to have died out also. This is an universal rule everywhere. The freeman never has any such light-hearted moments as the *Saturnalia* of the slave.

Of the true Americans, the "dark Americans" of the hymn, the old inhabitants of the continent, I saw but little. And what little I saw certainly disappointed me. I saw a good many young Indians in the Indian school at Carlisle in Pennsylvania. To the zeal, energy, and benevolence of all who are concerned in the work there I must bear such witness as I can. And I am told that the children are intelligent and take kindly to the civilized and Christian teaching which is set before them. But, just as in the case of the negroes, I could not keep down my doubts whether mere school-teaching will ever raise the barbarian of any race to the level of Aryan Europe and America. Of the two one is more inclined to hail a man and a brother in the Indian than in the negro. The feeling seems instinctive. While no one willingly owns to the faintest shade of negro descent, every one is proud to claim Pocahontas as a remote grandmother. Such Indians as I saw, the boys and girls, youths and maidens, of the Carlisle school, were certainly less ugly than the negroes. But then they lacked the grotesque air which often makes the negro's ugliness less repulsive. From my preconceived notions of Indians, I had at least expected to see graceful and statuesque forms, the outlines perhaps of nymphs and athletes. But the Carlisle Indians, clothed and, according to all accounts, in their right minds, seemed to me, both in face and figure, the dullest and heaviest-looking of mankind. Not repulsive, like the negro, from the mere lines of the face, they were repulsive from the utter lack of intellectual expression. Besides the younger folk at Carlisle, I was casually shown at Schenectady, in the State of New York, a man who, I was told, was the last, not of the Mohicans, but of the Mohawks. He was outwardly civilized, so much so indeed that the justice of the State had more than once sent him to prison. The mind, or at least the press, of America was just then very full of an English lecturer whose name was largely placarded on the walls, and whose photographs, in various attitudes, were to be seen in not a few

windows. I was not privileged to obtain more
than a passing glimpse of either. But it struck
me that between the survival of an old type and
the prophet of a new there was a certain outward
likeness.

During the time of my visit to America neither
the negro nor the Indian was the subject of any
vexing question. But the position of another class
of barbarians—I must be allowed to use the word
in a way analogous to its old Greek use—was under
the grave consideration of the federal legislature.
While I was in America, President Arthur vetoed
the first Chinese bill of last year; after I came to
England he passed the second. Of this latter bill
I do not know the terms; the President could
hardly have helped vetoing the former one, as its
terms were surely inconsistent with that famous
amendment which may be summed up in the
phrase of "giving everybody everything." Yet
I could not keep down a certain feeling of rejoic-
ing over either bill. I saw in them a practical
revolt against an impossible theory, a confession
of the truth that legislation cannot override natural laws. A constitutional amendment, or any
other piece of law-making, may in theory place all
races and colours on a level; it cannot do so in practice. An acute American friend pointed out to

me the distinctions between the three races which give rise to the difficulties that beset the United States in this matter. The Indian dies out. The negro is very far from dying out; but, if he cannot be assimilated by the white man, he at least imitates him. But the Chinaman does not die out; he is not assimilated; he does not imitate; he is too fully convinced of the superiority of his own ways to have the least thought of copying ours. The Chinese, in short, in the United States belong to one of those classes of settlers who form no part of the people of the land, who contribute nothing, but who swallow up a great deal. Now, at the risk of saying what I suppose is just now the most unpopular thing in the whole world, I must say that every nation has a right to get rid of strangers who prove a nuisance, whether they are Chinese in America or Jews in Russia, Servia, Hungary, and Roumania. The parallel may startle some; but it is a real and exact parallel, as far as the objects of the movement in each case are concerned. The only difference, a very important difference certainly, between what has happened in Russia and what has happened in America consists in the means employed in the two cases. What has been done in Russia by mob-violence is doing in America in a legal way. Now no one can jus-

tify or excuse mob-violence in any case, whether
aimed at Chinese, Jews, or any other class. But
any one who knows the facts will admit that Rus-
sian violence against Jews, though in no way to
be justified or excused, is in no way to be wondered at. And it is well to remember that,
though anti-Chinese action in America now goes
on in a perfectly legal way, yet there have been
before now anti-Chinese riots in California, as
there have been anti-negro riots in New York.
One thing I am certain of, namely that, if the
press of England, Germany, and other European
countries, were as largely in Chinese hands as it
is in Jewish hands, we should have heard much
more than we have heard about anti-Chinese action in America and much less about anti-Jewish
action in Russia. Just now there are no tales of
mob-violence against the Chinamen to record, yet
it would be easy for a practised Chinese advocate
to make out a very telling story about American
dealings with Chinamen. "Frightful Religious
Persecution in the United States," "Legislation
worthy of the darkest times of the Dark Ages,"
would have made very attractive headings for an
article or a telegram describing the measure which
passed Congress last year. No one has raised the
cry of "religious persecution" in America, because

there is no powerful body anywhere whose interest
it is to raise it. But it would be just as much in
place in America as it is in Russia. Neither the
Jew nor the Chinaman is attacked on any grounds
of theological belief or unbelief, but simply because
the people of the country look on his presence as
a nuisance. But the Jew has brethren from one
end of the world to the other, ready and able to
give his real wrongs a false colouring, ready and
able to make the mass of mankind believe that he
is, not only the victim of unjustifiable outrage,
which he undoubtedly is, but the victim of religious persecution in the strict sense, which he
certainly is not. The Chinaman has no such advantage. His case therefore has drawn to itself
very little notice out of America, and neither in nor
out of America has it been, like the Jewish case,
judged on an utterly false issue.

The difference between the position of these questions in America and in England illustrates in an
instructive way the difference between a scattered
and a continuous dominion. The different classes
of British subjects are yet more numerous and varied than the different classes of American citizens
and of dwellers on American territory without the
rights of citizenship. A black Prime Minister, a

yellow Lord Chancellor, of Great Britain is in theory
no less possible than a black President of the United
States. The real likelihood may be about equal on
both sides, but the theoretical possibility is forced
on the mind in the United States in a way in which
it is not in Great Britain. If a British subject of barbarian race seeks to take a share in the affairs of the
ruling island, he must cross a wider expanse of sea
than that which separates America from Britain ; he
must learn a strange tongue, he must adapt himself
to strange manners, he must become in everything
another man. To the negro citizen in America
everything is at least geographically near. He lives,
it may be, within sight of the Capitol and the White
House ; his kinsman under British rule lives far
away indeed from the Palace of Westminster. To
the American negro the tongue and the manners of
the ruling race are in no way strange ; they have
been, from his birth upwards, his own tongue and
his own manners, so far as the distinction planted by
the hand of nature has enabled him to attain to them.
It follows therefore that questions like those of the
Indian, the negro, the Chinaman, while they touch
the American at his own hearth, in no way touch us
at our hearth, deeply and sometimes grievously as
they touch us in our colonies and dependencies. The
Irish question alone is common to the two branches

of the English people. And it is plain that the Irish question takes two different shapes on the two sides of Ocean. The United States, happily for them, are not burthened with the hard necessity of providing for the government of a land where it seems impossible to do real justice. On the other hand, the problem of the "Irish vote" and its effects on home politics, though of growing and very unpleasant importance in Great Britain, is certainly not as yet of so great importance as it is in America. The Irish, as an element which can affect and sometimes turn an election, are in England confined to particular towns and districts : in America they seem to be everywhere. The influence which they obtain in local politics is really amazing. The "bosses," as they are called—a name of which one soon comes to feel the meaning, though it is rather hard to translate into any other phrase—who hold so important and so anomalous a place in the municipal affairs of American cities are largely Irish. On the whole, even setting aside the way in which Irish influence in America bears on us at home, that influence does not seem to be a healthy one. The position held by the Irish and the negroes made me feel more and more strongly the danger of that hasty and indiscriminate bestowal of citizenship which has become the practice, and rather the pride, of the United

States. The ancient and mediæval commonwealths, aristocratic and democratic alike, erred in the opposite direction. But one is sometimes tempted to doubt whether their error was not the smaller of the two. There is surely something ennobling in that kind of national family feeling, that cleaving to descent from the old stock, which was as strong at Athens and in Uri as it was at Corinth and at Bern. And surely a mean might be found between the exclusiveness of the elder commonwealths and the excessive lavishness of the younger. Surely birth in the land might be taken as the ordinary standard, a standard to be relaxed only in the case of eminent service to the commonwealth. As for the Irish, it is whispered that they somehow contrive to obtain citizenship yet more easily than the easy terms on which the law gives it. It is a characteristic story how the Irish immigrant was asked, before he had landed, what side in politics he meant to take—how his first question was, "Have you a Government here?"—how, being assured that the United States had a Government, he at once answered, "Then set me down agin it."

XI.

I must here say a word or two on ecclesiastical matters in the United States, so far as I can do so without straying on any fields of controversy which are better avoided. One coming from England, specially one coming from the rural parts of England, is struck in many ways by the fact that he is in a land in which all religious persuasions are on a footing of perfect equality. That fact strikes him in the mere appearance of the religious buildings. There is nothing in size or architectural character to distinguish the places of worship of any particular religious body. If there is any real exception to this rule, it is to be found in one very modern class of buildings. A church which shows any near approach to the character of a great European church is pretty sure to be Roman Catholic. But churches of this class are sure to be new, and are often unfinished. Built mainly by the offerings of the poor, no buildings anywhere do more honour to those who have reared them; still one cannot quite stifle a feeling that they are not in their right place. The great metropolitan church at New York, the lesser, but still stately, building at New Haven, must, after all, rank with the " bosses" and the other signs of Irish intrusion. They are not the genuine growth of the soil, like an Episcopal church in Virginia, a Congregational church in Connecticut, or a Roman Catholic church at Baltimore or at St. Louis. They lack antiquity, even in the modified sense in which antiquity is to be understood in the United States. For there is a standard of antiquity, even in the United States. It is wonderful how easily our standard in such matters shifts. As we count things ancient in England which we do not count ancient in Italy, as we count things ancient in Italy which we do not count ancient in Greece, so we gradually come in America to see a kind of relative antiquity in things which in England we should hardly call old, much less ancient. Everything older than the War of Independence, house, church, or anything else, has a kind of flavour of age about it. It belongs to a past state of things, and it carries about it the air of belonging to a past state of things. If it can boast of little positive beauty, it has at least the negative merit of being free from the worse uglinesses of modern affectation. A church of this kind is likely to belong to one of those religious bodies which once were dominant in different States, as Congregational in New England, Episcopal in Virginia. But in the great modern cities the English visitor is likely to be struck with the long rows of churches side by side, belonging to various religious bodies, but with nothing about each to show that it belongs to one religious body rather than to another. This is a novel feeling to one mainly used to the villages and old towns of England; but he may nevertheless have come across phænomena of the same kind in his own island. In many of our great modern towns, say in the academic quarter of Manchester, we see churches, Established and Non-established, side by side, with very little to distinguish them. So in Scotland, if the Established church can be distinguished from its rivals, it is not commonly by its greater architectural splendour. Still, taking England and America as wholes, this outward equality of the places of worship of all religious bodies is one of the things which decidedly strike as signs of the New World.

Indeed to one used chiefly to the older parts of England the indiscriminate use of the mere words *church* and *clergyman* has an unusual sound. But the changes in the use of those and kindred words are worth noticing, both in England and in America. Within my memory the most familiar names for Nonconformist places of worship have changed more than once, just as the name " Nonconformist" itself has displaced " Dissenter." The " meeting-house" has given way to the " chapel," and the " chapel " is fast giving way to the " church." The " chapel " has always struck me as a rather meaningless stage, and in New England, where the same change of name has taken place, it has been dispensed with. In the days when Congregationalism was the Established religion, each independent *church* met in its *meeting-house.* The *church* was not a building, but a society of men; the *meeting-house* was the place where the *church* met. In the like sort, I have a vague remembrance of some ancient Greek Father, who argued that the proper name for the building was not *ekklêsia* but *ekklêsiastêrion.* In old England the name *meeting-house* always had a slight savour of scorn about it; in New England it was used of choice as an honourable name by the dominant religious body of the country. The use of the word " church," if it has not come in since Disestablishment, has certainly strengthened since that time, and I suspect that its use, like that of " clergyman," has in it something of conscious assertion of equality all round. As the Roman Catholic speaks most naturally of his " priest," the Congregationalist or Presbyterian speaks most naturally of his " pastor" or " minister," and I venture to think that to the untutored Church of England mind no name comes so kindly as the " parson." But there is perhaps about the " parson" a certain savour of tithe and glebe which may not be altogether in place in an unendowed or disendowed body.

To one who is old enough to have marked for himself the great changes which have taken place in England during the last forty or fifty years, both in the Established Church and among Non-

conformist bodies, the inside of an American
church, whether Episcopal or otherwise, most commonly suggests that he has come among a highly
conservative people. I do not say always; sometimes an American church shows devices which
are altogether modern, but which are nevertheless
of a kind which certainly calls for our admi-
ration. I lectured in the Baptist church at
Brooklyn. The building, to my mediæval eye,
seemed more like an amphitheatre than a church;
but in one point the architect had done his work
to perfection. I never spoke in any building
where it was so easy to speak, and I imagine that
it was equally easy to hear. And this fact may
suggest a practical lesson. If a church is to be
simply a preaching-house, it is surely wiser to grapple with the fact, and to make a building which
thoroughly answers its purpose as a preaching-
house. It is well, in such a case, to cast away all
traditions, Greek, Roman, Anglican, or Lutheran,
which look on the church as something other
than a preaching-house. I lectured in some other
churches which did not answer their purpose so
well as the Brooklyn Baptist church, while they
had so much the general air of a Roman, Anglican,
or Lutheran church as to make one miss the altar at
the east end. This, I need not say I did not miss

at Brooklyn; there was nothing to suggest it. But this is not exactly what I meant when I spoke of conservatism in American churches. In several fashionable Episcopal churches I felt carried back to the days of my boyhood. All that we here rather pride ourselves on having got rid of since those days was there, flourishing yet more proudly than it flourished in England fifty years back. One sees a whole church filled with pews goodlier than any that could be seen in England even in that day, unless it were some gorgeous squire's closet which made the wretchedness of the rest of the building look more wretched still. American pews are velveted, chaired, stored with fans, provided with "all the comforts and conveniences as well as the necessaries of life." Above them soars the gallery, with its hired singers of both sexes, flaunting in the face of the congregation, just as they might be seen in an English town church fifty years back. At Newport in Rhode Island is a church, ancient according to the American standard, both in its fabric and in its fittings, and which is looked on with deep reverence because the organ was given by Bishop Berkeley. Things here differ a good deal from the fashionable splendours of New York; but they are quite as unlike anything that one has got used to in England during the last half-century. The pews seemed to be devised so as to cause every devotional act to be done under the greatest possible amount of difficulty. It was hard to listen, to worship, or even to sleep. Yet, after fourteen months, I remembered the sermon, as an instance of thoroughly good feeling thrown into a rather grotesque shape. The preacher told us his name and address at Charleston, South Carolina; he told his New England hearers how glad he would be to see any of them at his southern home, and he assured them that Garfield was as much lamented in South Carolina as he could be in Rhode Island. Such a church as this is a puzzle. The conservative American wishes to keep every pew as it is, on the ground of reverence for antiquity. The innovating Britisher, to whom the American's antiquity is newness, feels inclined to get rid of them on half-a-dozen grounds. In fact, in such a position as this, these ugly eighteenth-century boxes wake up the same kind of conflict and argument as those screens in some of our great churches which we feel would on every practical ground be better away, but against which we cannot bring ourselves to say a word because of their antiquity and beauty.

In all these matters the elder country has certainly been the more go-ahead of the two. May I

mention another instance of American ecclesiastical
conservatism, where I must be allowed to think
that British innovation has the advantage? I mean
the custom, which I noticed both in Episcopal and
other churches, of beginning to talk the moment
the service is over. In England we commonly wait
till we are out of the church. But the American
use is really a survival, a comparatively harmless
survival, of the practice of talking while the service
is going on. A long *catena* in favour of that practice might be put together, stretching from the
days of Edward the Confessor to those of George
the Third. Both in Britain and in America we
have improved since the days when Henry the
Second scribbled and looked at pictures all the time
of mass, since the days when Pepys and "the two
Sir Williams" had "much talk" in the pew. Still
I must think that Britain may claim the higher
praise, as having fallen away yet further from the
customs of those days than America has.

But the most amazing mixture of reckless innovation with something more than conservatism,
with deliberate falling back on the models of the
earliest time, is to be seen in the Prayer-book of the
American Episcopal Church. Every time I have
listened to it or looked at it, I have been more and
more amazed at the union of the two discordant

elements. It is easy to see historically from what quarters they severally came, but that makes it none the less wonderful that the same assembly of men, intrusted with the revision and alteration of a document, should have altered it in two opposite directions. The changes in the Morning and Evening Prayer and the changes in the Liturgy would seem to have been done by men ages or hemispheres apart. The one is mutilated and confused; the other is restored to primitive perfection. In the one, the object seems to have been carefully to destroy the order and harmony of the English book, and, at whatever cost, to turn good English into bad. In the other, the result has been to bring those fragments of antiquity which are all that either Wittenberg or Canterbury or Rome has kept back again to the full measure and beauty of earlier models. In the lesser office some needless and barbarous departure from a venerable pattern grates every moment on the ear. In the greater we feel carried into a distant and an elder world; by the banks of the Hudson and the Potomac we seem carried away to the Bosporos and the Dnieper; we feel how truly the far West has fallen back upon the teaching of the changeless East, when, in the newborn city or in the half-reclaimed wilderness, we seem to join with John Chrysostom, with Phótios, and with

Nikôn, in a rite which would not be out of place
beneath the cupolas of Constantinople or of Kief.
In the American Church every one accepts, no one
quarrels with, a formula which I can well believe
that British ignorance would call " Popish," because
it is of a truth the most speaking protest against
the Pope and all his works. We know, as a matter
of fact, that the disfigurement of the Morning and
Evening Prayer, alike in matter and in language,
simply represents the taste and feeling of the latter
part of the last century, while the restoration of the
ancient Communion-service was due to Bishop Sea-
bury's dealings with the Scottish Episcopal Church.
But this does not make it any the less wonderful
that men who could devise or put up with the
changes in one way could welcome other changes of
a kind so opposite.

With other forms of religious worship I was less
at home. I must confess that I generally find
extempore prayer unpleasant. It is commonly
accompanied by the lack of all sacerdotal pretensions; yet it always has to me a certain savour of
priestcraft. In an Anglican, a Roman, an Ortho-
dox, church, if I only understand enough of the
service to follow it, I am something. I am part of
a body whose doings are regulated by law, and not
by the arbitrary will of a particular man. In a

Presbyterian or Congregational church I am a dumb dog; I am at the mercy of another man, who can put up what prayers he chooses in my name, without my having any part or lot in the matter. At the same time I cannot but see the occasional advantages of a more flexible kind of worship. It is indeed easy to find a psalm to suit any occasion of life, public or private; but one can do so only with a certain feeling that we are perverting the meaning of the psalmist. I confessed myself half converted to extempore prayer when a minister prayed very intelligibly for the patriots of Crivoscia, and I could not but admire the discretion of a college chaplain who not only returned thanks for past benefactors but prayed for new ones. I was of course not surprised to find the ecclesiastical phraseology of some of the American religious bodies differing a good deal from anything to which I was used; but an "adult gents' bible-class," which I saw announced on the door of a very respectable church in a city of which my memories are the pleasantest, was something for which I was not prepared.

I am thus far speaking of sober and reasonable worship among men of our own race and colour. But in some parts of my journey I was able to get glimpses of something different. A camp-meeting

I did not see; but I did see one kind of worship which seemed to me passing strange. In my sojourn in rural Virginia I had the opportunity of seeing some illustrations of the law by which religion so largely follows race. As there is a Greek, a Latin, and a Teutonic Christianity, to say nothing of the Churches of the further East, so the black man has developed something for himself which is surely neither Greek, Latin, nor Teutonic. In the neighbourhood where I was staying, there was an Episcopal and a Presbyterian church, neither of them great works of architecture, but respectable buildings according to rural American notions. Between these more sober places of worship the white population was divided; and there was a pleasing simplicity in the sight of carriages and horses left freely about while their owners attended the service. But the negroes had places of worship of their own, Methodist and Baptist, not "steeple-houses" like those of their white neighbours, but huts hardly to be distinguished from their own cabins. I did not make my way into any of them; the undertaking seemed somewhat wild and perilous; but at Baltimore I attended two negro churches of quite opposite persuasions. One was Methodist, a building of some size, closely packed with a zealous congregation. I could have wished that the congregation had been less zealous or less closely-packed; for I should have greatly liked to stay to the end, which I found it utterly impossible to do on purely physical grounds. The praying, singing, preaching, was all of a kind which sounded very strange to me; but at least nothing could be more hearty. The sermon treated largely of Herod the Great; I trust I do not misrepresent the preacher when I say that, according to the memory of more than one hearer, he told us that the will of that prince was "taken to Rome to be *probated* by Augustus"—some thought he said by "a justice"— "before the Sanhedrim." From this scene I turned to another, which I understood better, a negro Episcopal church, with tendencies to what is called an "advanced ritual." It was but a little flock that was gathered together; but the few that there were seemed just as zealous as their Methodist neighbours. And I thought I could understand that these two seemingly opposite kinds of worship might easily commend themselves to the same class of minds. In both there is a greater opportunity of joining "lustily and with a good courage" than there is in some intermediate kinds of devotion.

There are however some black religionists who seem quite able to give a reason for the hope that is in them, but who would certainly not approve of

the small Episcopal flock and hardly of the larger
Methodist body. I read in an American novel a
negro theological poem, which seemed to be genuine, and which discussed the merits of various religious persuasions. I was sorry to find near the
beginning the lines—

> 'Piscopalians dey won't do;
> Dey fiddle and dance de whole night froo.

I do not remember the exact words of the rest;
but Presbyterians would not do either, nor yet
Congregationalists, nor indeed any sect except the
Baptists, who were exactly the right thing. But I
am afraid that in the verses that I quoted the negro
satirist hit upon a truth. In several of the great
cities—not in all—the Episcopal Church is very
distinctly the fashionable Church. I could wish
it were otherwise. I should think that to be a
merely fashionable Church was the very worst
thing that could happen to any religious body.
Better surely even to " die of dignity," as the
Church of England was said to be doing at the
beginning of the present century. One sign of
this unlucky position may be seen in the constant
reference to an ecclesiastical season of which in
England we hear much less. One whose creed
certainly did not commit him to its observance

warned a friend who was coming from England that he would hear the word "Lent" oftener at Baltimore than he had ever heard it in his life before. And he might have said the same of New York and Philadelphia. The penitential season certainly does make its mark in America in a way which we do not see in England. It does make a distinct break in that wonderful round of gaieties in which the great American cities seem to delight. One cause indeed may be, as was suggested to me, that the fashionable seasons of England and America are different. The rank and fashion of the older country does not shut itself up in a town till the country is putting forth its full beauties, that is, till Lent is over. America keeps different times, times which, if people are to be shut up in a town at all, are surely more seasonable, and times which Lent more distinctly breaks in upon.

But the existence of a fashionable Church, whether Episcopal or otherwise, in no way hinders the general equality of all religious bodies. The general good feeling about such matters strikes the visitor, and strikes him pleasantly, at every turn. If people in America despise or quarrel with one another about religious differences, they contrive to do it privately, and not to let the stranger see. It is a little odd to hear a bishop addressed by a

Quaker as " Friend A. ;" but it may well be the better for both bishop and Quaker. But I may notice one thing which I heard from an eminent Congregational minister, who, after a sojourn in the United States, was going back to England. He complained that the clergy of all religious bodies in America were more closely confined by public opinion to their strictly religious duties than they are in England, either in the Established Church or among Nonconformists. He gave a curious and amusing instance. Soon after he settled in America, he was invited to attend a public meeting. He naturally thought that he would be asked to make a speech, to propose or second some resolution. But no; all that fell to his lot was to share with another minister the duty of saying a kind of grace before and after meat, while the real work of the meeting was assigned to laymen only. And in other things he complained—and his complaints, like all other things, got into the New York papers —that he was cabined, cribbed, confined, in his sphere of action in New York in a way in which he was not in London. He was expected to mind his own business in a way to which he was not used in England. Yet the position of a popular preacher in an American city certainly seems to be both an influential and a profitable one, and my

Congregationalist friend was perhaps not worse off than English bishops of ordinary sees are said to be in the House of Lords, if they ever venture to obey the Queen's summons, and to take their part in the general affairs of the realm.

I need hardly tell any one that there is not now, in any State of the Union, what is commonly understood by an Established Church. How an Established Church is to be defined is perhaps less easy to rule than many people think. And I sometimes gratified my love of paradox by saying that in the United States it would be truer to say that there are many Established Churches than to say that there is none. That is to say, though no religious body is in any way dominant, in any way favoured by the State, yet any religious congregation can easily obtain legal incorporation, and a position which may really be called State establishment, though assuredly without endowment. When I say without endowment, I mean of course without endowment granted by the State; for endowments of other kinds the State protects. Some people seem to think—perhaps they would not say so in so many words, but practically they think—that by disestablishment and endowment a religious body will wholly escape from State control. The records of American law courts would soon

undeceive them. There are in truth two quite distinct forms of interference in ecclesiastical matters
on the part of the State. There is the personal
supremacy of the Sovereign, as acknowledged by
the Established Church of England, and exercised
at present by the Queen in Council. This is the
supremacy of the Sovereign as Supreme Governor
of the Church, and it is equally the supremacy of
the Sovereign, whether those who act as the Sovereign's advisers in its exercise are lawyers, or
bishops, or anything else. To this supremacy of
course there is nothing answering in the United
States. But besides this there is the general supremacy of the law, exercised by the ordinary courts
of law; and this supremacy must be exercised in
some shape in any country where there is any law
at all. From this supremacy no person or society,
secular or spiritual, established or disestablished,
can escape. And this supremacy is constantly
exercised in ecclesiastical matters by the American
courts. Almost any question of doctrine or disci-
pline in any religious body may come before a
temporal court, because every such question may
involve a question of contract. Take such a case
as this, the proceedings in which I read while in
America. A Roman Catholic priest was dismissed
from his cure by his bishop. Such dismissal of

course touches both his reputation and his pocket, and, if done wrongfully, it is a civil damage. Whether it is done wrongfully or not depends on the question whether it is done according to the regulations of the Roman Catholic Church, which both bishop and priest have contracted to observe, and which, as a matter of contract, the temporal law will enforce against both of them. What the regulations of the Roman Catholic Church on any matter are becomes a matter of evidence. In the case of which I speak the settlement of this point involved a disputation in canon law which might have called forth the learning of all Doctors' Commons when Doctors' Commons still was. To enable the Court to decide whether the Bishop's act was regular or not, the counsel on each side quoted endless canons of endless councils, from the œcumenical assemblies of the early Church down to the decrees of a provincial synod held a few years before in their own State. Proceedings exactly the same in principle may happen in the case of any other religious body; only there is something specially curious when one finds the temporal court of an American State listening patiently to arguments founded on the decrees of councils held ages back at Trent or Lyons or Rome. This kind of jurisdiction, though exercised under different forms, is essentially the same as that which is exercised when the King's Bench—or whatever now answers to the King's Bench—sends a *mandamus* to any ecclesiastical judge, ordinary, or visitor. It is a jurisdiction which must, in some shape, exist in all times and places; it is a jurisdiction which the pagan Emperor Aurelian exercised between two claimants for the possession of a Christian church. It is a jurisdiction which in our own country affects Nonconformist bodies just as much—though by a somewhat different procedure—as it affects the Established Church. It flourishes in full strength on American soil, and it there produces a class of cases which for me, at the time of my visit, had a special interest. The supremacy of the Crown has gone, and has left no representative; the supremacy of the law is as strong there as ever.

XII.

The Universities and Colleges of the United States, and the general position of the country with regard to learning, formed a subject which naturally attracted a good deal of my thoughts. I was thrown more among members of the American colleges than among any other class of people, and certainly from no class of people have I ever received more kindness than from some of their presidents and professors. One of the first things that strike the stranger is the amazing number of universities and colleges. It is said that in the one State of Ohio there are thirty-two institutions that grant degrees. We can hardly be wrong in inferring that the degrees granted by some of these institutions cannot be worth very much; it is quite certain that some of them are institutions of quite another kind from acknowledged seats of learning like Harvard and Yale. And perhaps we should not be wrong if we were to infer that it would be a gain if some of these degree-giving bodies were abolished or merged in others. We are sometimes amused at home at the ease and coolness with which any new-made school, without the least shadow of a collegiate foundation, dubs itself a " college." We are more seriously provoked when an ancient foundation which has lived on for ages under the honourable name of " grammar school" thinks it fine to deck itself out with the silly title of " college" or " college school." But these " colleges" at least do not call themselves Universities; they do not profess to grant degrees. It is allowed that for the exercise of this last power a royal charter must be had. Now my feelings make me most loath to say a word in any federal country against the powers of the several States; but it is surely not unreasonable to hint that the right of granting degrees should be assumed only by authority of the federal power. For a degree is surely a national thing, or rather it is something more than a national thing. It ought to be—I do not say whether it anywhere is—something like knighthood in old times, a badge of scholarship which should enable a man to take his place among scholars in any land to which he may come. On the other hand, the smaller and less distinguished American colleges are not a mere unmixed evil. If they largely hindered men from going to the better colleges, then they certainly would be so. But from all I could gather, the choice commonly was, not whether a lad should go to Harvard or Yale or to an inferior college, but whether he should go to the inferior college or should get no education at all. In this latter case it is to be supposed that some little knowledge, some little culture, is gained, which may at any rate be better than none at all. And I can say from my own knowledge that there are American colleges of much less reputation than the great ones where there certainly are good teachers, and therefore, I presume, good teaching. The course of my journey led me to a good many of them; and everywhere I found some one, or more than one, whom I was

glad to meet and should be sorry not to meet
again.

Looking at the colleges at the whole, or rather
at what may be supposed to be the effect of their
teaching on the general cultivation of the country,
the fault or danger seemed to me to lie in a certain
tendency to mediocrity, a tendency not to go to
the roots of things. I speak only by comparison.
Such tendencies are certainly familiar enough
everywhere; they certainly cannot be called an
American peculiarity; it may be going too far to
call them even an American characteristic. For
the state of mind of which I speak, though it
was brought forcibly to my notice on the other
side of Ocean, is only too common in England
also, and in many parts beside. I remember years
ago acting as Examiner at Oxford with a man
who, whatever may have been his attainments as
a lawyer, had certainly made a good deal of
money at the bar. He made the men who were examined say that the Conqueror introduced the
feudal system at the Great Council of Salisbury.
I implored him to say nothing of the kind, and explained to him that the legislation of Salisbury was
the exact opposite to what he fancied. My col-
league refused to hearken; he had to examine in
law; Blackstone was the great oracle of the law;

Blackstone put the matter as he put it, and he could not go beyond Blackstone. This is an extreme case of a man who cannot get beyond his modern book, and to whom the notion of an original authority is something which never came into his head. I can speak only of my own subjects, but I should suppose that some analogous state of things is to be found in other branches of knowledge. At any rate there is in all parts of the world a large class of people into whose heads it never does come that history is written from original sources. I have had talks with people, and have received letters from people, who clearly thought that I or any other writer of history did it all from some kind of intuition or revelation, who had no idea that we got our knowledge by turning over this book and that. And I have known others who have got beyond this stage, who know that we get our knowledge from earlier writings, but who fancy that these earlier writings are something altogether strange and rare, the exclusive possession of a certain class, and placed altogether out of the reach of any but members of that class. They are amazed if you tell them that for large parts of history, for all those parts at any rate with which I am mainly concerned, the sources lie open to every man, and that the only advantage which the professed historian has is the greater skill which long practice may be supposed to have given him in the art of using the sources. Now this state of mind, one which practically does not know that there are any sources, common enough in England, is commoner still in America. There, if we except a small body of scholars of the first rank, original sources seem to be practically unknown. It struck me that, with regard to reading and knowledge—at least in those branches of which I can judge—America stands to England very much as England stands to Germany. I conceive that in Germany the proportion of those who know something is smaller than it is in England, while the proportion of those who know a great deal is certainly larger. Anyhow this distinction is perfectly true between England and America. There is a mysterious being called the "general reader," of whom some editors seem to live in deadly fear. Now I had long suspected that the "general reader" was not so great a fool as the editors seemed to think, and my American experience has confirmed that suspicion. America strikes me as the land of the "general reader;" and, if so, I am not at all disposed to think scorn of the "general reader." It seemed to me that in America the reading class, the class of those who read widely, who read, as far as they go, intelligently, but who do not read deeply—the class of those who, without being professed scholars, read enough and know enough to be quite worth talking to—form a larger proportion of mankind in America than they do in England. On the other hand, the class of those who read really deeply, the class of professed scholars, is certainly much smaller in proportion in America than it is in England. The class exists; it numbers some who have done thoroughly good work, and others from whom thoroughly good work may be looked for; but it sometimes fails to show itself where one might most have expected to find it. Men from whose position one might have expected something more seem hardly to have grasped the conception of an original authority. One sees college library after college library which does not contain a volume of the Chronicles and Memorials, where the existence of that great series seems to be unknown. I met men who admired Dr. Stubbs as they ought to do, who had read his Constitutional History carefully, but who had never so much as heard of those wonderful prefaces, those living pictures of men and times, on which, even more than on the Constitutional History, the fame of the great Professor must rest. How little some men, even in the chair of the teacher, have grasped the nature of the materials for historic study came out in a curious dialogue which I had with an American professor, I think a professor of history. He asked me, " Where do you write your works ? " " In my own house, to be sure," I answered; " where else should I ?" " O but you can't do them in your own house ; you can't have the rare books and the curious manuscripts; you must be always going to the British Museum." He was a good deal amazed when I explained to him that all the important books for my period were printed, that I had them all around me in my own not wonderfully large library, that it was the rarest thing for me in writing my history to need a book that was not in my library, that I had never in my life made use of the British Museum library, and not very often of the Bodleian --that, for a few unprinted manuscripts which I knew would be of use to me, the British Museum would give me no help, as they did not happen to be there—that, as a mere affair of the pocket, it was cheaper as well as more convenient to buy books for oneself, and to have them at home, than to take long journeys in order to read other people's books elsewhere. All this seemed altogether a new light to my friend. Of course a student of some other periods could not have made the same answer that I did. There are times for which the library of the British Museum, or in its measure any other public library, must be invaluable; but those times are not

the eleventh and twelfth centuries. But it is plain
that to my professor all centuries were much alike;
he knew that there were such things as original
sources, but they seemed to him to be something
strange, mysterious, and inaccessible, something
of which a private man could not hope to be the
owner. That a man could have the Chronicles and
Florence and Orderic lying on his table as naturally
as he might have Cæsar and Tacitus had never
come into his head. I heard a good deal in America
of the difficulty of getting books, which I did not
quite understand. It is surely as easy to get a book,
whether from London or from Leipzig, in America
as it is in England; the book simply takes somewhat longer to come. But I can understand that
American scholars may keenly feel one difficulty
which I feel very keenly too. This is the utter
hopelessness of keeping up with the ever-growing
mass of German books, and yet more with the still
vaster mass of treatises which are hidden in German
periodicals and local transactions. Of all of these
every German scholar expects us all to be masters,
while to most of us they are practically as inaccessible as if they were shut up in the archives of the
Vatican. When a German, and yet more when a
Swiss, scholar gets any fresh light, his first impulse
is carefully to hide it under a bushel, and then he

expects all mankind to enter in and see the darkness.

I think I may fairly say that the state of things of which I speak, not so much mere ignorance of original sources as failure to grasp the existence and the nature of original sources, while sadly rife in England, is yet more rife in America. But I need hardly say that America has men of sound learning in various branches of knowledge of whom no land need be ashamed. At Harvard, at Yale, at Cornell, the most fastidious in the choice of intellectual society may be well satisfied with his companions. There, it is hardly needful to say, he will find thorough masters of not a few subjects, some of them indeed men of world-wide fame. It would be invidious to mention names, and some of them are of the nature of that good wine which needs no bush. The systems of the two most famous of these institutions differ a good deal, and I had several opportunities of hearing the competing merits of Harvard and Yale set forth by vigorous champions of each. Yale, the younger institution of the two, boasts specially of standing fast in the old paths, and of chalking out definite roads for both teachers and learners. The pride of Harvard is to give its students the widest freedom in the choice of subjects, and its professors the widest freedom in the

way of dealing with them. I have had more opportunity of judging of the teachers than of the learners ; but, as far as I can venture to judge of the matter, I should be inclined to say, Let both systems go
on side by side, and let each develop itself as it best
may in its own fashion. In our own island it would
be a distinct loss if either the English Universities
took to imitating the Scottish or the Scottish Universities to imitating the English. And so I imagine that, within the bounds of the United States
and even within the bounds of New England, room
may be found both for the system of Harvard and
for the system of Yale. There is life too and vigour in some of the younger institutions. Good
work is done on the hill of Ithaca, so lately a wilderness, where the academic colony of Cornell looks
down on lake and village at its feet. And I might
go on through other institutions in various places,
where, besides finding a kindly welcome, I greeted
here a scholar, there a lawyer, there a divine, who
might hold their own on much more famous spots.
Nor must I pass by without a word the two great
female colleges of Vassar and Wellesley, rival institutions, so say their enthusiastic scholars, after
the type of Harvard and Yale. I saw something of
Vassar, and I have heard much of Wellesley, which
I was unluckily hindered from visiting in the body.

Wellesley boasts itself of more strictly carrying out its own principles and more rigidly shutting out the ruder sex from its rule and teaching. One thing is plain, that both colleges are set down in most pleasant and healthy spots, with every opportunity of training the body as well as the mind. But, from what I have seen and heard, I cannot keep down a little doubt whether the mind is not overtrained. Girls who are at all eager to learn are generally very eager indeed, and it struck me that some of the subjects were rather too advanced for the years of the learners. Perhaps I have no right to speak; for one subject at least was far too advanced for me, and I fancy for a good many others. From the discourse of a (male) professor of rhetoric I carried off one phrase, the "œconomy of interpreting power," which I have found no one on either side of Ocean able to explain to me. In my secret heart I cherish the hope that it may be high-polite for the wise precept of Mr. Chucks in "Peter Simple"—"Spin your yarn in plain English."

It must not be forgotten that many of these colleges and other public institutions are fruits of that personal munificence of which America can boast no small share. The chaplain who prayed for fresh benefactors was not praying for any miracle. The spirit of the old founders of monasteries, colleges, hospitals, schools, lives on in the newer England with a more plentiful life than it now keeps in the older. Nor is it only the easy munificence of the last will, munificence at the cost, not of the man himself, but of his natural successors. Not a few of these modern founders have, like their elder fore-runners, lived to see their own creations working. And many of those creations keep some very direct, and sometimes rather strange, marks of the founder's personality about it. It is, for instance, a strange restriction at Girard College, Philadelphia, which forbids any minister of religion, of whatever persuasion, so much as to set foot within the walls. But this shutting out of the ministers of religion does not shut out religion itself; there is a chapel, and worship is carried on in it. The two great colleges, open to all persuasions, alike for teachers and learners, have yet each a dominant theology and a dominant worship. Unitarianism is in the ascendant at Harvard, Congregationalism at Yale. But each is simply in the ascendant; no one need accept the theology of the place; only such is the theology of the place for such as accept it. Cornell takes a wider range. There is a large chapel with a smaller one built on to it; in the latter the service of the Episcopal Church is regularly said by a professor who is an Episcopal clergyman; in the main chapel ministers of all denominations, invited by the President, take their place in turn. The Roman Catholic Bishop was invited among others; but he pleaded that the laws of his Church did not allow him to accept the invitation.

I need hardly say that in none of the American universities or colleges, any more than in the bodies which have of late taken the name of colleges among ourselves, do we find the ancient collegiate system, as understood at Oxford and Cambridge. It seems as hard to make an American as it is to make an European continental understand the nature of the single university with its many colleges. I saw a book of travels in England by an American professor, in which, after a fairly accurate description of Cambridge and what was to be seen there, including of course the several colleges, he wound up, "The formal style of *Cambridge College* is 'the Chancellor, Masters, and Scholars of the University of Cambridge.'" I have sometimes tried to explain the matter both to American and to Swiss hearers by bringing in the analogy of the Union and the States. Historically the analogy is false; for the Union is an union of States, while the University, older than the colleges, is certainly not an union of

colleges. Practically there is a good deal of likeness. Each college, like each State, manages its in-
ternal affairs, but a single college can no more confer
a degree than a single State can make war or peace.
An American college too has nothing answering to
the Master, Fellows, and Scholars of an English
college. The Fellows, the kernel of the society,
are absent; the name is sometimes known, but,
when it is known, it means members of an external
governing body. Of the many names for the head
to which we are used, President is in America almost universal, though there is a Chancellor of an
University at St. Louis and a Provost (not of a college or university) at Baltimore. The title of President seems indeed to be the favourite in America
for all purposes. In England, setting aside the
great officers of state and justice who bear it, we
seldom give it to the head of any body which is not
in some way religious, benevolent, literary, scientific,
or artistic; we never, I think, give it to the head of
a purely commercial body. But in America we
find the President of a railroad and the President
of a bank—that is, what we should call by the
simpler name of Chairman. In the working of the
colleges I suspect that an academic antiquary would
find out that, among some novelties, some old things
have been preserved. All the colleges seem to have

a course of four years, and the students of the four years are Freshmen, Sophomores, Juniors, and Seniors severally. The question at once starts itself, Why is the "Junior" so called in his third year and not in his first? The answer is that "Junior" and "Senior" are short for "Junior Sophist" and "Senior Sophist." We have here in short the *Generalis Sophista*, the man of two years' standing who has passed his "responsions," who was not quite forgotten at Oxford in my younger days, and who, I believe, is better known both at Cambridge and at Dublin. The "Sophomore," who sounds as if he were a wise fool, a follower of James Sixth and First, is more puzzling; but I believe he is not an American invention; traces of him have been found by curious eyes on this side of Ocean also. The odd thing is that these same names are used in the girls' colleges also, and moreover a young lady becomes in due time Bachelor and Master of Arts. I was a little puzzled by the strong tie, expressed by the name "classmate," which is held to exist between men who have entered college at the same time. I could not remember anything the least like it at Oxford; when I came to think, I remembered that my most intimate friends did not happen to be men of exactly my own standing, but men a little older or younger.

But it really only answers to the Cambridge phrase of "men of my year," which I believe is looked upon as a tie of some strength. Still I never fully grasped the idea of the "class" and the "class-mate;" and I still do not understand how all the men of the same year, who must differ vastly in abilities and attainments, can be driven with any profit through the same course. Some other phrases that puzzled me I came more easily to understand. I was startled by hearing a young man saying that he had to go to his "recitation;" it gave me the idea of a little boy repeating "My name is Norval." But I found that a "recitation" was much the same as what I should understand by a "college lecture"—I mean as college lectures were forty years back—and I feel sure that the name is not a new one. "Commencement," the great academic ceremony of the year, bears a name which is unknown at Oxford, but which is perfectly familiar at Cambridge.

The time of the year at which I was in America did not enable me to see a college commencement; but I fancy it must be a scene of a good deal of interest. At Harvard I was told that the Governor of Massachusetts comes out with an escort of fifty horse, himself in plain clothes, but with aides-de-camp in splendid uniforms. He is, I fear, received by an University in plain clothes. Any academic garb, as a regular thing, seems to have quite vanished, though I came to one or two colleges where the students themselves were making praiseworthy efforts to revive the use of the square cap. Nor is the ancient statute of Yale College now observed, which required a student to make obeisance if he came within a certain measured distance of a professor, and which forbade him to come at all within a certain smaller measured distance. But that was in days when Yale taught the Ptolemaic astronomy, which it certainly does not teach now.

But, while speaking of the American colleges and the general intellectual culture of the country, there is one case in which I must stop to make a more special mention. There is a school of American scholarship growing up, whose researches come specially home to me. Students of early English history and language have had of late to acknowledge much valuable help in several shapes from the western branch of their people. But the school of which I have to speak is one which, among its other merits, has the special merit of being distinctively American, of being the natural and wholesome fruit of American soil. Its researches have taken that special direction which one might say that American research was called upon to take before all

others. The new school is the natural comple-
ment of an elder school which has been useful in
its time, but which could at the utmost serve only as
the pioneer towards something higher. I mean
the school of the older local historians of America. Even from the days before independence, such
local writers have never been lacking. Every State,
every district, almost every township, has found its
chronicler. And worthily so ; for every State, every district, every township, has its history. In
New England above all, the history of even the
smallest community has some political instruction
to give us. The history of New England is a
history of exactly the same kind as the history of
old Greece or of mediæval Switzerland, the history
of a great number of small communities, each full
of political life, most of them reproducing ancient
forms of Teutonic political life which have died
out in the elder England and which live only
among the lakes and mountains of the elder
Switzerland. The institutions of any community
in the Thirteen Colonies, above all of any community in New England, are more than a mere
object of local interest and curiosity. They show
us the institutions of the elder England, neither
slavishly carried on nor scornfully cast aside, but
reproduced with such changes as changed circum-

stances called for, and those for the most part changes in the direction of earlier times. As many of the best reforms in our own land have been— often unwittingly, and when unwittingly all the better—simply fallings back on the laws and customs of earlier times, so it has specially been with those reforms which were needed when the newer England arose on the western shore of Ocean. The old Teutonic assembly, rather the old Aryan assembly, which had not long died out in the Frisian sea-lands, which still lived on in the Swabian mountain-lands, rose again to full life in the New England town-meeting. Here we have, supplied by the New England States, a direct contribution, and one of the most valuable of contributions, to the general history of Teutonic political life, and thereby to the general history of common Aryan political life. And other parts of the Union also, though their contributions are on the whole of less interest than those of New England, have something to add to the common stock. Each of the colonies reproduced some features of English life ; but different colonies reproduced different sides and, so to speak, different dates of English life. All these points in the local history of the colonies need to be put in their right relation, both to one another and to other English, other

Teutonic, other Aryan, institutions. This would seem to be a study to which the scholars of the United States are specially called. The study of institutions, the scientific exposition of what America has to teach us on that head, has been taken up by those who have come in the wake of the older school of American inquirers. On the more homely researches of the local chronicler has naturally followed a newer and more advanced class of inquirers, men who not only collect facts, but who know how to put the facts which they collect into their proper place in the general history of mankind. A young and growing school, which still has difficulties to struggle against, may be glad of a good word on either side of Ocean. I cannot help mentioning the school which is now devoting itself to the special study of local institutions, a school which is spread over various parts of the Union, but which seems to have its special home in the Johns Hopkins University at Baltimore, as one from which great things may be looked for. Nor can I help adding the name of my friend Mr. Herbert B. Adams as that of one who has done much for the work, and who, to me at least, specially represents it. To trace out the local institutions, and generally the local history of their own land, to compare them with the history and institutions of elder lands, to show that it is only on the surface that their own land lacks the charm of antiquity, is the work which seems chalked out for the inquirers of this school, and a noble and patriotic work it is. An eye accustomed to trace the likenesses and unlikenesses of history will re- joice to see the Germans of Tacitus live once more in the popular gatherings of New England—to see in the strong life of Rhode Island a new Appenzell beyond the Ocean—to see the Great City of Arcadia rise again in the federal capital by the Potomac. North and South, and the older West also, has each its help to give, its materials to furnish. Viewed rightly, with the eye of general history, it is no mean place in the annals of the world that falls to the lot of the two great commonwealths between which the earliest, and till our own days the greatest, presidencies of the American Union were so un- equally divided.

XIII.

I now come to some more strictly social matters. Of "society" in the technical sense, the sense which gives rise to the odd New York phrases of "society woman" and "society girl," the "society" whose doings are so diligently and wonderfully recorded in the New York newspapers, I do not suppose that

I saw very much. I should doubtless be out of place among those who

"Fiddle and dance de whole night froo,"

whether the fiddling and dancing is or is not the outward sign of any particular theology. I received a great deal of very kind hospitality, both at New York and in other places, and I made many acquaintances which I hope to keep; but I do not presume to think that I penetrated to the centre of social, any more than of political, life. And I confess that the thought has sometimes come into my head whether a city like Bern or Athens, which is the political centre of a people, but where " society," in the sense which that word bears in London and New York, does not exist, really loses anything by the lack of it. And the thought has also come into my head, whether, supposing " society" to exist, a court or something like a court—notwithstanding all the manifold evils of a court—may not have its good side. But these are abstract speculations. Of the wonderful goings on at those gatherings where each young man is expected to give each young woman a nosegay worth a man's ransom I cannot speak from my own knowledge. Of more sober dinners and other receptions I might say a good deal; but at such entertainments, often got up specially for a stranger, one can judge but imperfectly of the way in which people live among themselves. But I may notice, and I have heard the same remark from others, that immediate national politics seem not to form so constant a subject of discourse in America as they do in England. This, I suppose, has something to do with the same set of causes which has given the word "politics" the special and not altogether pleasant meaning which it bears in America. The divorce between politics and society, or indeed between politics and the higher culture, strikes one very strongly. It may be one of the weak points of a federal system that the highest range of politics is not so directly brought before every man as it is in a kingdom or commonwealth of another kind. The questions which come more immediately before him, the politics of the State or the city, may well have a side which is repulsive to the cultivated man; and the result may be that federal politics themselves fall too largely into the hands of a class of professional "politicians." The difference between paid and unpaid members, paid and unpaid officers of various kinds, must also make a difference. The ideal state of things would surely be one in which the members of the legislature should neither be paid nor be called on to pay.

Mr. Bryce pointed out not long ago (" Fortnightly
Review," November, 1882) that what are commonly
thought to be the evils of American political life
are neither so great nor so universal as they seem.
Still there is in America a divorce between political
and social life ; and the federal system may well be
one cause of it, both by hindering the existence of
a real capital and in other ways. I have remarked
something of the same kind in Switzerland.   There
too national politics seem not to occupy men's
minds in the same way in which they do in England.   The President of the Swiss Confederation is
a much smaller person than either the American
President or the English Prime Minister, for the
obvious reason that the power which most nearly
answers to the President or the Prime Minister is the
Federal Council as a whole, and not its chairman
personally.   Still it seemed to be odd that very intelligent people in Switzerland were sometimes not
able to say offhand who was the President of the
year.   Anyhow, whatever may be the cause, it is,
to say the least, unlucky when any class, above all
when the most cultivated class, shrinks from political life or ceases to take an interest in political
affairs.   If politics are rougher in America than
they are in England, if they are likely to be rougher
in England than they have been hitherto, that is

no real reason for shrinking from them, but the opposite.

But it is on some other and smaller aspects of American life that I wish now to speak. I have noticed at one or two earlier stages the way in which the British visitor is struck with the constant absence of ceremony on public occasions where we should have looked for some measure of form and state. There seems, for instance, to be a general dislike to the wearing of any kind of official dress. In matters of this kind I fancy that a good deal has been consciously dropped out of a notion of "republican simplicity." This is a feeling which I cannot enter into. Whatever honour a free commonwealth shows to its chosen magistrates is surely honour done to itself. If I were to speak of the magistrates of old Rome, with their lictors and their official ornaments, I might be told that Rome, if a commonwealth, was an aristocratic commonwealth. But there never was a purer democracy than that of Uri, and the Landammann of Uri keeps—at least he kept eighteen years back—no small measure of official state. And indeed, even in the United States themselves, some degree of official pomp cannot be got rid of on all occasions. I have mentioned the Governor of Massachusetts as keeping some measure of dignity about him; I saw

the late Governor enter his capital, undecorated
certainly as far as his own person was concerned,
but otherwise surrounded by a degree of pomp and
circumstance which reminded me of the triumph
of Marcus Furius Camillus. And, in private life,
the American strikes me as, on the whole, more
ceremonious than the Englishman on this side of
Ocean. I do not profess to know how far this may
be owing to the absence of acknowledged artificial
distinctions, but it seeems not unlikely that the two
things may have something to do with one another.
It certainly did strike me on the whole that, among
those with whom I had to do in America, there
was not less, but more, attention paid to minute ob-
servances than there is in England.

But here again our universal rule steps in. In
some cases certainly the difference is due to the
fact that England has dropped ceremonial usages
which have lived on in America. Take for instance the commonest forms of address. The
British visitor in America is a little surprised at
being called "Sir" in private life, at all events at
being called so a great deal oftener than he ever is
in his own island. The word perhaps grates a little
on his ears. But he has only to turn to his Bos-
well to see that America has in this small matter
simply kept on an usage which England has

dropped. And this is a matter in which England stands almost alone in the world. The Frenchman, at all events, has his "Monsieur," "Madame," and "Mademoiselle" ever on his lips, in a way which the Englishman finds it a little hard to follow. In England we seem to have a growing tendency to get rid of the vocative case altogether. And in the many cases when a man is not quite sure what is the right formula to use, when, for instance, he is inclined to familiarity but is not quite sure whether familiarity will be welcome, it is wonderful how long he may go on without ever using the vocative. And, without going to this extreme, it is certainly not thought elegant in England to indulge very greatly in its use. No one wishes his name or title to be brought in with every breath. But in America, besides the use of "Sir" in a way which has died out in England, no one can fail to remark the supposed necessity of giving everybody some kind of title. Now it must always be remembered that the strongest sign of an inherent love of titles is to be found, not in the use of titles like Duke, Bishop, General, but in the use of plain "Mr.," "Mrs.," and "Miss." The higher titles are not mere titles; they state a fact about the man to whom they are applied; they tell you that he is a bishop, a duke, or a general. But "Mr.," "Mrs.,"

and " Miss" tell you nothing; they are used wholly
to avoid the supposed impropriety of calling people,
as of old at Athens and now in Iceland, simply by
their names. In America it is distinctly harder
than it is in England to get people with whom you
are really intimate to drop the " Mr.," and use simply the surname. And I noticed that men who
were thoroughly intimate with one another, men
who were old friends and colleagues, spoke of and
to one another with handles to their name, in a way
in which men in the same case would not do here.
On the other hand, men are constantly spoken of
in the newspapers by their mere Christian and surnames in a way to which we are not used in print.
But in my own experience it was a relief when I
escaped with simple " Mr." I generally had to
writhe under the ugly titles of " Professor" or
" Doctor." Why anybody should mistake me for
a professor, or why anybody should thrust the title
of " Doctor" on the bearer of a purely unprofes-
sional and honorary degree, was beyond my understanding. I asked not uncommonly whether they
talked of " Dr. Gladstone." In one famous university town I was able to turn the tables on my
friends, and to ask them why they should either
call me " Professor" or wish to be called " Professor" themselves, when there was in their own

city a "Professor Parker," showing off dancing dogs. In some parts a stranger is commonly addressed as "Colonel" or "Judge." I was never addressed as "Colonel," save once at Baltimore, and that in the dark; so it was hardly because of any specially military air about me. "Judge" I never was called; though, as I happen to have something to do with judging, while I have nothing to do with teaching, it would have been one degree less out of place than "Professor." But, though these queer titles are a little trying to a stranger, the application of them is thoroughly well meant, according to the custom of the country. It seems as if no one in America could do without some kind of handle. We are used to "Governor A.;" but "Mayor B." and "Minister C." sound to us odd. But more than once, when I had been introduced to "Governor A." and had put myself into a proper mood of respect towards the chief magistrate of the State, I found that all that was meant was that the gentleman to whom I was speaking had been Governor in times past. In language that is at all precise it is counted more correct to say in such cases "Ex-Governor"—as if one should say "Ex-High-Sheriff B."—but the "Ex-" is certainly often dropped. And the title given to the husband often extends to the wife. I have seen "Mrs. Professor"

on a lady's card, and the newspapers sometimes tell
one how "Mrs. Ex-Senator A." went somewhere
with her daughter "Mrs. Senator B." Nor is it
always easy to remember all among the large class of
people who are called "Honourable;" and I found
that "Esquire" as an address was chiefly applied to
lawyers. Among these, by the way, the formula
"Attorney- and Counsellor-at-law," preserving two
names which in England have perished, is quite the
right thing. I was little surprised at the vanishing
of "Esquire." "George Washington, of Mount
Vernon, Esq." was a description with which I was
quite familiar, and I had often seen the title "Esquire" in American books and stories. But there is
a trace of its earlier use in the phrase commonly
used in some States of "being brought before the
squire," meaning before a magistrate of any kind.

Now this lavish use of titles is universal; so it
is to be supposed that people like it. Yet in one
most distinguished University I was told by more
than one professor that he liked better to be addressed simply as a gentleman, or better still as
a man, without any official title. But the really
important point is that, in this matter also, American usage is older than English usage, and is certainly more consistent. We have the practice of
other European nations against us. Thick on the

ground as handles are in America, they are still thicker in Germany, and they are much more freely extended to men's wives. Then in America and in Germany the thing is thoroughly carried out; in England it is hard to find out the principle on which the handle is sometimes used and sometimes not. As to the wives, our rule seems to be that, while any kind of rank which is strictly personal, whether hereditary or otherwise, any rank from duke to knight or even esquire, is shared by the wife, strictly official rank is not. The dignity of the bishop, the judge, the sheriff, is not shared by his wife. Yet there is one notable exception. The Mayoress, in London and York the Lady Mayoress, has her undoubted place, and in London at least the dignity is transferable; the Lady Mayoress may chance to be, not the wife, but the daughter or sister, of the Lord Mayor. Now "Mrs. Professor" sounds very ugly to us; but in Germany "Frau Professorin" is universal, and it is hard to see how she differs in principle from the Lady Mayoress. Then again it sounds odd to British ears to hear a young lady spoken to or of by any one above the rank of a servant or other inferior as "Miss Mary." But this again was once universal, if not with the modern "Miss," yet certainly with the older "Mistress." This last form at least is graceful, and so it sounds in some other tongues, in Greek above all.

If there is any rule of precedence in private American society, I was not able to catch it. But I was once a little amazed at the question of a most cultivated American lady, one who knows England well, whether in England any one who might be supposed to be at all personally known did not feel annoyed at being placed after a man of higher rank who had no claim to distinction beyond that of being of higher rank. In England, where the virtual ruler of the country holds a formal position far below many whose higher position is his own gift, the thought probably never enters into any man's head. I could only tell my questioner that I could not answer for others, but that such a thought had certainly never come into my own head. I said that I no more thought of repining because A. or B. was of higher rank than myself than I thought of repining because he was younger or taller or handsomer than I was. In either case facts are facts, and the facts are no fault either of his or of mine. I told her that in such a case no kind of wrong was done, no affront was meant or thought of on either side, that the whole thing was a matter of course, like an order of nature, of which nobody thought at all. But I found that the American lady did not in the least enter into my feelings.

The rare use of the word " esquire" may have something to do with the total, or nearly total, disappearance of the thing. There certainly once were country-gentlemen in the North as well as in the South. The "Patroon" is gone ; but his memory is not forgotten; and the Patroon was not a solitary being, but the chief member of a class. That the class should die out is not unnatural where the law of equal division exists ; yet in France some relics of the class do continue to linger on in spite of it. And, from a hill in New England which commanded a wide view, a local friend pointed out two houses the owners of which he said still kept up something of the position of English squires, and were popularly called by that title. Still such cases must certainly be exceptional. American life, as a rule, centres in the towns; indeed many Americans seem unable to understand any life which does not centre in a town. In my own case most people seemed to assume that I must live either in London or in Oxford, or, as some, I know not wherefore, suggested, in Manchester. The idea that a man, at all events that a man who wrote books, could live in his own house among his own fields seemed altogether strange to them. It is not

that there are no country-houses in America; very
far from it; he who can afford it has both his
country-house and his town-house. But he who
cannot afford both has his town-house only, and
with him who has both the country-house is quite
subordinate to the town-house. The town-house is
the real home; the country-house is merely the
place for an occasional sojourn. A rich man, say
at New York, who could afford to make, if he could
not find ready made, the stateliest of parks and
country-houses, prefers to build a grand house in a
New York street, while his country-house is an
altogether secondary matter. And the country-
house again is very often not quite what we should
understand by a country-house in England. It
often comes nearer to the nature of a "villa;" it
often has neighbours too near to it to be altogether
the real article. The lack of real country-life is
shown by some of the forms of summer relaxation
in America. "Camping-out" in the wilderness
doubtless has its pleasures, but it is more likely to
suggest itself by way of violent contrast to the inhabitant of a town than to one whose daily portion
lies among woods and fields of some kind. The
feeling of the rich American seems to be altogether
different from the feeling of most men in England,
whether of inherited or of acquired wealth. The

one has already, the other buys or builds, his house in the country. He doubtless has his town-house too; but it is his country-house which comes first and is really his home. The English gentleman is Mr. A. of such a place in the country, who most likely has his house in London also. The American gentleman is Mr. B. of such a city, who most likely has his house in the country also.

In this matter of town and country, the vast extent of the United States combines with their political constitution to cause another difference between England and America. In England we have only one centre, that wonderful something—for a city we cannot call it in its aggregate—which is at once a political, a social, and a literary centre. London has lately been taught that, in a political sense, it is not England; but it none the less is, and it more and more thoroughly becomes, the one centre of England. Neither the Universities nor the great commercial cities—and there is now happily one English city which may claim both names—are centres in the same sense. Purely local centres, neither academical nor commercial, some of which still held their place a hundred years back, have, as centres, simply vanished. London keeps its old place, and it has taken the place of the local centres as well. But no one American city can, as things now stand, take the place which London holds in England. For no American city is at once the greatest city in the land and at the same time the seat of the national government. To make an American London, New York and Washington must be rolled into one. But New York and Washington rolled into one would not really make an American London. The size of the country, its federal constitution, would, either of them alone, be enough to hinder any city from becoming the one real national centre, like a great European capital. No city can be a real national centre to people who live three thousand miles off. Even if it could be so for political purposes, it could not be so for social purposes. And under a federal system, where each State does for itself so large a part of what we should call national business, the central attraction is necessarily divided. If no place within the State can be all that a national capital is in an ordinary kingdom or commonwealth, so neither can any place out of the State. And when, as in many States, old and new, the State capital is not fixed in the greatest city of the State, the attraction is divided again. Philadelphia certainly remains the head of Pennsylvania in a sense in which Harrisburg is not. It remains the head of Penn- sylvania in a sense in which we can hardly believe that even York and Exeter ever were the centres of their several counties, in a sense in which they certainly have long ceased to be their centres. In England therefore there is but one centre; in America there are many. In England we may say that, setting aside London and a few towns of special character like Brighton, Bath, Cheltenham, no one lives in a town unless he has some business, official or professional, which makes him live there. In America, on the one hand, men live in towns who have no official or professional necessity to live in them, and on the other hand the professional and mercantile classes necessarily hold a higher comparative position in America than they do here. Every large town therefore becomes a social centre in a way in which it cannot be in England. New York has one kind of attraction, Washington has another; but the whole country does not press to either of them in the way in which all England presses to London, and to London only. London is something different in kind from any other English town; New York is simply another American town on a greater scale. It must never be forgotten that New York, though it calls itself a "metropolis," though I have even known its newspapers sneer at the rest of the country as "provinces," is in no sense a capital. So far from being the capital of the United States, it is not even the capital of the State of New York. It is simply the biggest town in the State and in the Union. Washington, as the seat of the federal government and the dwelling-place of foreign ministers, is something different in kind from any other American town; but then it has not enough of size or importance in other ways to make it a general centre. One sees this in the newspaper press. Owing to the multiplicity of centres, no American papers can hold exactly the same position as the great London papers. But it is clearly the New York papers which come nearest to it; the Washington papers one looks on as simply local, more local a good deal than those at Chicago.

Now it strikes me that, if the dominant life of a country is to be its town life, it is a great gain that there should be many centres of such life, and not one only. And in America there is no danger of its being otherwise. New York certainly takes a great deal upon itself; but the other great cities are quite able to hold their own against it. Neither old Boston nor new Chicago looks on itself or on its State as a " province" of New York. And we must also remember that, from one point of view, town life is, after all, not dominant in the

United States. It is dominant in the point of view which chiefly strikes such a traveller as myself. He misses the country-houses, the manor-houses and parsonages of his own land; his friends, old or new made, are sure to be mainly in the cities. But he must not forget that, in American political life, the cities are by no means exclusively dominant. If America has few squires, she has plenty of yeomen, and those on a magnificent scale. If in one way the American cities count for far more than the English cities, if from one point of view America seems to be all town and no country, from another point of view the country counts for far more than it does in England. At any rate the real voice of its inhabitants counts for far more.

Now this predominance of town over country, so far as it exists, is one of the points in which America does not, as in so many others, cleave to an earlier form of English life. There undoubtedly was a time when the old towns of England—as distinguished from the great commercial centres, new or of new growth—counted socially for more than they do now. And yet, when this was so, London itself, from some points of view, also counted for more than it does now. But there never was, or well could be, a time when social and intellectual life in England had so many centres as it now has in America. Still, if America in this respect does not reproduce an older England, it has some likeness to the continent of Europe as distinguished from England. Even in France, and of course far more in Italy, the old local capitals still hold a place which we may safely say that no town in England but London ever held since there was any united England at all. We must remember that, if Paris is, in many points, in all the most obvious points, far more thoroughly the centre of France than London is the centre of England, there are other points, less obvious but not without importance, in which it is less so. For instance, we might almost say that no book is published out of London. Books are still published in the Universities, in the Irish and Scottish capitals; but those who publish them find it needful at least to have London agencies. Now France is not quite like Germany in this matter; still good books are published in other French cities besides Paris. It was perhaps an exceptional case when I met an intelligent Norman gentleman who had never been at Paris, who indeed had never been out of Normandy in his life. But I could hardly fancy an Englishman in his position who had never been in London. So again I have known foreigners show a little amazement at hearing that it was now an unheard-of thing for an English nobleman or country gentleman to have his town-house in any town except London. I need not say what the use of Italy is in this matter; even in France, where any *noblesse* is left, the town-house in the old capital of the province is still not uncommon. Indeed it strikes one on the continent that everybody likes, if he can, to have two dwellings, to have a town- and a country-house, even if the one be a garret and the other a hut. But the town-dwelling comes first; town-life is the thing taken for granted. I have myself found German scholars, not less than American scholars, puzzled at my not living in a town; they seemed unable to conceive any one living in the country in any position between the *Junker* and the *Bauer*. In all this, if America has departed from the model of England, she has conformed much more to the model of the rest of the world. It is the insular branch of the English folk which is in this matter the peculiar people.

The great American cities, those which have taken their position as centres of life for large parts of the country, contrast remarkably with the smaller towns and villages. In this matter, as in so many others, whatever in America is not palpably new is pretty sure to be genuinely old. A small

American town or village—in some States the
name "village" is the legal description of what
we should call a market-town—one that has not
grown with the same speed as its greater neighbours, is apt to have a very old-world air indeed
about it. I am not speaking of new and unfinished
places in the more lately settled States, some of
which have a very desolate look. I mean towns
dating from the earlier days of settlement, but
which have failed to advance with their neighbours,
even if they have not positively gone back. I
remember very well the general effect of Bristol in
Pennsylvania. If the younger Boston and the
younger York have greatly outstripped their older
namesakes, the younger Bristol has as distinctly
lagged behind the older. It had once, I believe, a
considerable trade, which is now swallowed up by
Philadelphia. It stands on a good site above the
Delaware, and it has altogether, as these older towns
commonly have, a respectable, comfortable, and
thoroughly old-world look. Places of this kind
have somewhat the same air as those open towns or
large villages which lie on what, in the days of
coaches, was the main road between London and
Oxford. I am not sure that the general impression
of belonging to a past state of things is not stronger
in the American than in the English places. This

feeling is perhaps strengthened by the contrast between these old towns and the extremely modern air of the great cities. And the constant use of wood in building houses, an use almost equally common in some parts of England, always gives an air of age. Let me speak of another place smaller than Bristol, one indeed which we should not call a town at all, but a large village of detached houses. This is Farmington in Connecticut. Here was a truly old-world place, and I was taken to see the oldest house in it. And it was a house which we should call old even in England, a respectable wooden house of the seventeenth century. It was just what a New England house should be, except that its grand old open fire-place was blocked up by some modern device or other. But, if the house was thus satisfactory, a turn of disappointment was caused by the discovery of the inhabitants. Not that I have anything to say against them; I doubt not that they are respectable and excellent people in their own way. Only their way was not the way that I came to look for. I came to see New England Puritans, and I found Ould Ireland Papishes. And unluckily the fate of this house is a typical one. It is a grievous truth that not a few New England houses are left altogether empty, while not a few others are occupied by Celtic strangers. The only comfort is that New England has gone westward. Those whom we ought to find in the old homes have gone, like their forefathers, to win new conquests for that strong English folk which called into being on their new soil institutions older than those of the England which they left behind them. But the immediate feeling at the change which has come over New England is a grievous one. I had to seek my comfort in a lower range of the animal world. It was cheering, after going a few yards, to fall in with something of so old-world an air as a yoke of oxen, and oxen too that seemed to have something of a Pilgrim-fatherly cut about them. Indeed at such a moment there was a measure of relief even in a most primitive kind of coach which took us back to the railroad. But, putting aside the intruders, both Farmington and Bristol are thoroughly old-world places. It is only by negative signs that the really modern date of an American town of this class gradually comes out. The general feeling of such a place is certainly older than that of an ordinary English market-town. But then the American place, though everything about it looks in a manner *old*, contains nothing that can be called *ancient*. The English town or village, on the other hand, while a great deal in it will be much newer than anything in the American town, will commonly contain some objects which are ancient, and not simply old. It will commonly have a church, it is not unlikely to have one or more houses, which carry us back to days far older than the Pilgrim Fathers. That is of course supposing that the church has not been restored, or that it has been restored with some degree of mercy. I have seen old-fashioned wooden churches in America, for whose details of course there was nothing to say, but whose general effect was a good deal more venerable than that of an ancient English church on which a modern architect has been let loose to play his tricks.

Of the newer parts of the country I saw but little, and of the rural parts of the older States not much beyond what I saw in my visit to a very retired part of Virginia. Here at least we were "remote from cities," more remote certainly than in any part of England that I am used to. But the state of things there is, I fancy, very different from the newly occupied settlements. Much as the land has suffered from the civil war, a civilization of two hundred and fifty years' standing is not altogether wiped out. A Virginian farm-house differs a good deal either from an English country-house or from a house in New York; but it is possible to live quite comfortably in it. The presence of an inferior race hinders much of the difficulty and discomfort which is found in the younger parts of the States. I heard of an English lady in Iowa who had to scrub her own floors; there is no such hard necessity in Virginia. Life, to the visitor at least, is not exciting; there seems to be little society, and a certain difficulty, which I never found in any other part of the world, in knowing what to do with one's time. It is a simple and uneventful way of living; but the main essentials of civilization are not lacking. It had however its disappointments. For I failed to see two things which I had fully hoped to come across, if nowhere else, yet at least both in Virginia and in Missouri. I saw none of the beautiful quadroons that I had read of in books. At every stage I was told that I should see them further south; but I suppose that I never got far enough south for the purpose. Still I do not understand why they should not grow at Baltimore or St. Louis, just as much as at New Orleans. I saw one colored woman who was not absolutely ugly, and she was in Connecticut. I was disappointed too in seeing next to nothing of the *fauna* of the country. The 'coons and the 'possums I was told I should see, like the beautiful quadroons, further south; but I never got far enough south to see them either. In

most parts of the country I was struck, a good deal
to my amazement, by that same lack of living
beings which has become usual in England and
elsewhere in Europe. In a visit reaching from
October to April I could not expect to see much of
insect life; but I did see the famous " katydid" in
Rhode Island, and she seemed, to the unscientific
eye at least, to be a close ally of the Italian *grillo.*
In the beautiful Druids Park at Baltimore I saw
the grey squirrel at liberty in the trees, and a
species of deer distinct from any of our three British kinds in that state of half-freedom which belongs to deer in a park. But, as I saw no 'coons or
'possums, I never saw even the pretty little ground-
squirrel with the striped back. In Virginia I sometimes saw in air the wild turkey who was presently
to appear at table, and I had good opportunities of
studying the manners and customs of the turkey-
buzzard. The turkey-buzzard, it should be remembered, has nothing to do with a buzzard, and still
less with a turkey; it is really a small species of
vulture. Its power of sight must be wonderful.
It is strange indeed to see the birds flocking together from all quarters to any spot where the car-
case is. There they crowd together and enjoy their
feast till they are disturbed—for they are easily
frightened, and fly off at the approach of a man—

or till they are so thoroughly gorged that they cannot fly off. They are so useful as scavengers that
the law of the State commonly protects them. I
do not know however whether the turkey-buzzards
have anywhere attained to the same rights as the
fish-hawks in New Jersey, who seem to form a
privileged order among all other animated creatures.
There, if I have not been misled, the very tree on
which a fish-hawk has once made its nest is sacred.

In this quiet Virginian life I said that the main
elements of civilization were not lacking. But I
must make one important exception. It is however an exception which has to be made in the case
of more thickly inhabited parts of America, and
even, in some sort, in the case of some of the greatest cities. I mean the utter absence of decent roads.
In the part of Virginia in which I stayed, you literally see the roads, in the words of the famous
rime, "before they were made." Neither Lee nor
Grant seems to have thought it needful to follow the
praiseworthy example of Marshal Wade. Walking,
riding, driving, are all done under difficulties, over
roads which have never been brought under the
dominion of the art of Appius and MacAdam. The
lack of good roads is a general feature wherever I
have been. I do not say that I saw no good roads

in America; but good roads certainly are exceptional. In many parts, as I before remarked, the
railroad has come before the road. Even in the
immediate neighbourhood of large towns, sometimes
even in the streets of large towns themselves, the
road is often simply a mass of mud. I do not mean
merely such mud as in many parts of England we
are used to after rain; I mean thick abiding mire,
abiding at least for several months together. In
newly settled places the street often consists of a
miry way in the middle, and a path of planks on
each side. And the path of planks is often seen,
even where things are in much better order than
this. The great cities vary greatly in this matter,
and New York is certainly not the best. The very
first thing that struck me on the day after landing
was the neglected and dirty state of many of the
New York streets, a state of which an English
market-town would certainly be ashamed. I ask
why so great a city is not better looked after in
so important a matter, and I am told that it is
owing to the corrupt administration of the Irish.
This may or may not be so; if it be so, it is surely
another argument against Irish ascendency. I
was told also that the Americans are a long-
suffering people, and I partly believe it. The
tendency to stand still sometimes strangely con-

trasts with the tendency to go ahead. Take for instance the post-office. Some of its arrangements are not a little behindhand. It seems wonderful that, while you may send a packet of manuscript at a low rate from Bagdad to California —I was going to say from Kamtschatka, only then it might perhaps go by way of Alaska—if the same packet is sent from one part of the Union to another, it is charged the full letter rate. That letters within the country, travelling as they do for distances so much greater than ours, should be charged somewhat more highly, is perhaps not unreasonable; but they might surely be allowed to be a full ounce in weight, as in England. Then again there is no place where it is so easy to post a letter as in an American town; there are street-boxes at almost every step. But to register a letter, or to go through any of the other branches of postal business, often calls for a long journey. I could not find out that there was more than one place in Philadelphia where a letter could be registered. If there is more than one—in a city greater than any English city except London—there certainly are wonderfully few.

Another strange lack in some of the greatest American cities is the want of any good system of hackney-carriages at moderate fares. In this matter it is perfectly true that a dollar in America goes no further than a franc in Europe. It would certainly cost several dollars to go as far in New York as you can go in Rome for a single *lira*. Here at least England is not singular; it is a general question between the old world and the new. Simply to get from one part of an American city to another is an object for which every provision is made, and often made in a way which is a triumph of enterprise and ingenuity. The cars climbing the inclined plane at Cincinnati are truly amazing, and in the descent at evening the view of the city is striking in no slight degree. The upstairs railway at New York is far more pleasant to the stranger than the underground railway in London; and I was told that those through whose streets it goes, who might have been expected to dislike it, are reconciled to it by its bringing them more custom. It would however be a gain if both the railway-cars above and the tram-cars below were hindered from taking more passengers than they are made to hold. And neither the tram-car nor the upstairs railway serves the exact purpose of taking you to a particular house, say, in the case which American hospitality makes a very common one, that of being asked out to dinner. Then you must either walk all the way or part of the way, often at the risk of some mud,

or else you must take a hired carriage at what to an
European seems an unreasonable cost. At New
York I was told that the Irish were at the bottom
of this also, as of most other things which either
natives or strangers complain of. But why should
transplanted Englishmen, or transplanted Dutchmen
either, bow down their necks to this Irish bondage?

XIV.

The railroad- and the tram-car in the cities suggest the wider use of the railroad in general American travelling. The traveller is soon made to feel
the vastness of the country by the familiar way in
which he hears people speak, and in which he presently comes to speak himself, of distances which in
Europe are quite exceptional. Three or four hundred miles go for nothing. During an adjournment
of two or three days in the State Legislature of
New York, members were running off to Buffalo
and back, as if it had been something like going
from London to Reading. To go from New York
to San Francisco is talked of as if it were no
greater matter than to go from London to Inver-
ness. I know not whether I ought to tell how one
gentleman did me the honour to come all the way
from Mobile to St. Louis, a distance about as far as
the whole length of Great Britain, merely to make

my acquaintance. I felt abashed, as I had certainly never taken such a journey to meet any continental or American scholar. And this feature of American life cleaves to the traveller when he comes to home; at least Carlisle no longer seems to me the distant spot which it did even a year ago. To my own mind, what was chiefly brought home by this light handling of distances was, not the vastness of the whole country, for which I was prepared, but the vastness of many of the States. I have not tried Texas, which is said to be about the same size as the whole dominions of the King of Hungary and Archduke of Austria; but New York among old States and Illinois among new fill a pretty considerable space on the map. Now in England we instinctively fancy that a State answers to an English county or a French department. And for some purposes it does. I had to maintain that proposition against an American author who thought me unreasonable for complaining that his country-men did not know the English counties. No one in England, he said, knew the counties in an American State; no one in America knew the counties in any State but his own; very often a man did not know the counties in his own State; sometimes he hardly knew the county in which he lived himself. I ventured, with my small American experience, to traverse his

fact. I could believe that in New England a man
might not know the county of his neighbour, that he
possibly might not know his own; but I told him
that in Virginia people knew their counties as
naturally as they do in England. But I argued
that, as regarded people in one country knowing
the geographical divisions of the other, to know
the county in England answered to knowing the
State in America. The county in the one case, the
State in the other, is the highest geographical division; it is that which stands out visibly on the
map; it is that which a man names when he is
asked in what part of the country he lives. Ask
the inhabitant of England where he lives, and he
names his county. Ask the inhabitant of the
United States where he lives, and he names his
State. I know one exception, but it is one that
proves the rule. Many years ago I was sitting at
dinner in Oxford next to an Episcopal clergyman
from America. He talked to me freely on secular
politics, and the word " State" often came into o ir
discourse. Presently our conversation was broken
in on by another guest asking my neighbour from
what part of the United States he came. I saw
how in a moment he took the measure of his questioner: he marked a clerical coat, waistcoat, and
tie; his voice and look became quite different from

what they had been while engaged in worldly talk
with me, and he answered that he came from the
diocese of New York. But I conceive that, in
speaking to any one in a lay garb, even this canny
divine would have defined his dwelling-place by his
State. In a purely geographical aspect then the
American State does answer to the English county;
the wide difference in the political position of the
two is of no importance when we are simply map-
ping out the surface of the land. To know an
American county answers rather to knowing English poor-law unions or petty-sessional divisions,
which no one out of their immediate neighbourhood can be expected to do.

But if the English county does, for simple geographical purposes, answer to the American State,
American travelling soon brings home to us how
very different a thing in point of extent an American State is from an English county. Without
going off into the wilds, a journey through such
States as New York and Pennsylvania does indeed
impress us with a feeling of the vastness of those
commonwealths. Still there is another way of
looking at the matter. Shallow people laugh at
small commonwealths, whether in old Greece or in
modern Switzerland. And I have known New
York papers laugh at Delaware; I know not

whether any one, even in New York, is so hardy
as to laugh at Rhode Island, where the spirit of
Roger Williams still abides in the very dogs.
Shallow people ask what instruction there can be
in the past history or present politics of commonwealths so small as those of Greece or Switzerland;
above all, they ask what can be learned from commonwealths which had no printing, no railroads, no
electric telegraphs. The political thinker will
rather hold that the small commonwealth, with its
stronger and fuller flow of life, is more native, more
typical, and therefore richer in real instruction,
than the large state ever can be. He will hold
that the political advantage of modern inventions is
that they go far to raise the large state to the level
of the small one. No modern community can ever
be like the Athenian democracy; but the inventions of modern skill, the printing-press, the railroad, the telegraph, by the improved means of
communication which they give, go far to enable a
large state to get over the disadvantage of its size,
and to put its citizens somewhat more nearly in the
position of the men who hearkened to Periklès.
We may be quite certain that, without these modern
inventions, so vast a Confederation as the United
States could not be kept together; with them, its
members are practically brought as near to one an-

other as were the cities of old Achaia. To travel in the United States, to communicate with ease with every part of its vast area, and indeed with lands beyond the Ocean, brings forcibly to the mind how our world has grown in physical size since the days of old Greece, and also how modern skill has equalized the physically great and the physically small. The most startling thing in the way of communication that I ever saw was when the President's message appeared in the New York papers accompanied by the comments which had been already made on it by the London papers. The difference of time between England and America allows this to be done easily; and it may comfort us of the old world with the thought that there is after all some advantage in living nearer to the rising of the sun.

But I have been carried off from the immediate subject of American travelling. I need hardly dwell on the various small peculiarities by which it is distinguished from European travelling. I have already hinted that some of the peculiarities of the American railroad-car will not be new to any one who has travelled in Switzerland, and that some of them are finding their way into the railroads of our own island. Two reforms I might suggest; a better supply of porters, especially at the smaller stations, and the getting rid of the men and boys who are allowed to go up and down the cars with books and fruit, who leave you hardly a quiet moment, and who almost hurl the last new magazine at your head. But against my fellow-passengers I have nothing to say on any of my journeys. I have never been hailed as "stranger"; I have never, on land at least, fallen in with the pushing, questioning, fellow-traveller, a dim tradition of whom we are apt to take out with us. As for the American hotel, it is not an inn, but an institution. No one really knows how to keep an inn so well as a Frenchwoman, a Frenchwoman in a steady-going old French town uncorrupted by tourists. To her you stand in a very different relation from that in which you stand to an American "hotel-clerk." But let us do justice to the hotel-clerk, as to all other men. The relation in which you stand to the French landlady is a domestic relation; that in which you stand to the American hotel-clerk is a political relation. To the one you are a guest, though a guest that pays; to the other you are, I will not venture to say a fellow-citizen, but at least a protected subject. No one in the world teaches you your place so well as the American hotel-clerk. For my own part, I have little or nothing to com-

238 IMPRESSIONS OF THE UNITED STATES.

plain of on the score of mere civility. But the
civility of the hotel-clerk is a stately and lordly
civility, such as one might conceive a well-disposed
Czar or Sultan showing to the meaner class of his
subjects. But I do not know that there is anything distinctively American in all this, though it
is thrust more strongly on our notice in America
than elsewhere. It is the natural consequence of
changing the hotel—a word which in itself is simply
French for the English "inn"—from a house into
an institution. Wherever this change has taken
place, whether in America, in continental Europe,
or in our own island, the same results follow. Instead of being looked after by the landlord or landlady as personal human beings, we find ourselves
units in a body politic, protected or oppressed by
the rulers of that body politic.

But there is no doubt that the hotel system has
found a greater developement in America than it
has in any part of Europe save those which are
infested by tourists. The thing which seems
strange to the British traveller is the way in which
American hotels are thronged by those who are
not travellers. What is the meaning of that cease-
less crowd which seems to choose the ground-floor
of the hotel to do everything, to read, to write, to
talk, to do all those things which, one would think,

might be more comfortably done at home? Loung-
ing quietly in a southern *café*, above all by an
Italian lake, undoubtedly has its charms; but what
can be the charm of a place where everybody is
pushing to and fro, like the crowd at an election,
only without anybody to elect? The "Ladies'
Entrance" no longer seems puzzling; it becomes
the natural way for quiet people of either sex.
Only it is a pity if it has suggested the special
"Ladies' Box" at the post-office, to which the untutored Englishwoman, expecting to find her own
and her husband's letters lying in close conjugal
neighbourhood, does not think of going till the
mystery is explained after many days. I never got
quite to the bottom of these sources of puzzledom,
any more than I could understand why many people in America really choose to live in hotels. But
perhaps it is a natural developement of the predomi-
nant tendency to town life. " I wonder what they
can find," says Hobbie Elliot, " to do among a
wheen ranks o' stane-houses wi' slate on the tap o'
them, that might live on their ain bonny green
hills." When a man who might live among his
own fields chooses rather to live in a street, it is
only going a step further to live in an hotel rather
than in a house of his own.

But the hotel and the railroad are only the means of travelling. The object of travelling is to visit this place and that, for whatever may be the purposes of the particular traveller. Now in American travelling there is much that is pleasing and instructive; but the chief charm of European travelling is not there. There is something very strange in going through a vast land in which there is not one ancient building, where no historical association can be anything like three hundred years old, where the chief historical associations are only one hundred years old. To be sure, you may here and there be shown a primæval monument, at whose date or at the race of whose builders you do not venture even to guess. But here extremes meet; a monument so old or so strange as to have no meaning teaches nothing. A work of an altogether unknown folk cannot rank with the stones of Tiryns and Còra. In central America indeed we used to hear of monuments which did teach something, buildings which might help, along with Tiryns, with Tusculum, and with Signia, to throw light on the great invention of the arch. And in the Smithsonian Museum at Washington I was shown an inscription which I certainly could not read, and which I was told that nobody else could read either. This at least raises curiosity; some day some one may be able to read it, and then something may be learned from it. But that, as a whole, the United States are a land lacking in antiquities hardly needs to be proved. In this, above all things, newness proclaims itself on the surface. It seems strange to pass on for a whole day, from town to town, without a glimpse of a single ancient work of any kind. And the newness of the land forces itself on the traveller in another way at which I have at once glanced for a moment. There is so little between town and town. In one sense, to be sure, there is a great deal; there is, for instance, the corn land of Illinois. But there is nothing like those unbroken signs of old habitation which show themselves at every step as we pass through most parts of England and of many other lands. The old-established village, the ancient church, the inhabited manor, the shattered castle, the monastic ruin, all the things that make up the outward history of an old country, all are lacking. The patriotic American will perhaps answer that his country is all the better from never having known some of these things; and, as far as the castles go, I shall certainly not dispute against him. But I am not speaking of the past or present welfare of the land, but of the look of the land in the eyes of the traveller who passes

through it. As I before said, we adapt our standard of antiquity to circumstances, and we may, by
an effort, reach the frame of mind in which the
mill at Newport, even without turning it into a
wiking's tower, becomes as Silchester or as Norba.
Nor is it only the lack of signs of ancient occupation that strikes us. The whole land, even in some
of the older States, has an unfinished look; it is
not thoroughly filled up; it is still in making; the
charred roots of the burned trees are of themselves
witness enough. In all these ways the newness of
the land makes itself known as we pass through it.
That there are old elements in the land also we shall
find out if we seek for them; but we have to seek
for them.

I sometimes stopped to think how strange,
looked at from an European standard, must be
the state of mind of an intelligent and well-read
man, who has used books and museums to good
purpose, but who never saw an ancient building,
who never saw an ancient object of any kind in
its own place. No European can be in this case.
If he has seen only the objects of his own country,
he has at least made a start; he has qualified
himself to compare the objects of his own land
with those of other lands; he is like a man who
has learned one alphabet, and has thereby qualified

himself to learn others. But we need not feel
any pity for our friend who has read and not seen.
In one point he has the advantage over us. We,
who have been used to ancient objects of some
kind from our childhood, can never feel anything
like that opening of a new world which must
come upon such a man as I have supposed when
he first sees an ancient work of any kind. We can
never taste the feeling. The first sight of a Greek
temple is thrilling ; but we have been in a manner
led up to it by the buildings of other lands. The
first sight of Rome is thrilling ; but we have been
in a manner led up to it by Eboracum and Lindum,
by Vienna and Arelate, by Augusta Treverorum
and Colonia Agrippina. But to the traveller from
the New World all is fresh. One is sometimes
inclined to regret that so many American travellers
get their first glimpse of anything ancient in so
comparatively poor a minster as Saint Werburh's
at Chester. But it is perhaps as well that Ely
or Saint Ouen's should not come first ; and, if they
really spell out the length and breadth of the City
of the Legions, if they do not simply look at its
head church and its rows, they have found no bad
introduction either to the Roman or to the Teutonic
world. My American friends who have seen Europe may be able to enter into my feelings when I

tell them that, notwithstanding all that they and
their land had supplied to win my regard, yet
before I left it, I not only began to feel a wish for
my own home, but also to feel a more general
yearning to be in any land, England, Italy, or any
other, where there was something old. It seemed
not to matter whether the old thing was a Cyclo-
pèan wall or a Perpendicular church-tower; anything that was not of yesterday, anything that had
a history, would fill up the blank.

Here then is the painful gap in American travelling. Still the lack of antiquity does not become
painful till we have got pretty well used to the
country. For a while the very lack has somewhat
of the charm of strangeness. And if there are no
old objects, there are plenty of striking new objects,
some which are really worthy of study. The position and look of some of the American cities is very
striking and stately. Cleveland by its lake, Cincinnati with the hills above its great river, St. Louis
rising above its yet greater river, would hold no
small place among the cities of the elder world.
So would the federal capital as seen from the Potomac, if only the hideous unfinished monument
could be got rid of. The "magnificent distances"
are filling up, and Washington, with the home of

the Union ending the long avenue with its mighty
cupola, is becoming no contemptible modern capital. And it fills one with simple amazement to see
the way in which a vast and stately town like
Chicago has risen from its ashes. In that great
city I could see or hear of nothing older than the
fire, save a church-tower which showed the marks
of fire at its angles, and a single detached wooden
house of an antiquated type. This last suggested
that Chicago before the fire was something widely
different from Chicago after it. Philadelphia on its
peninsula, though the peninsular site does not come
out quite like Bern or Besançon, affords some good
points of view. But on the whole the American
city which struck me most was Albany. Rising
grandly as it does on both sides of the noble Hudson, it suggested some of the ancient cities on the
Loire. It has the advantage, rather rare in American cities but shared with Albany by the federal
capital, of having one dominant building. The
general look of the city carried me so completely
into another part of the world that, if any one had
come up and told me in French, old or new, that
the new capitol was "le château de Monseigneur le
duc d'Albanie," I could almost have believed him.
This State capitol at Albany — why cannot it
have a more rational name, like the State-*house* at

Boston ?—finally settled, for me at least, a question
which I had been turning over in my mind ever
since I landed in America. This was, What ought
to be the architecture of the United States ? That
is to say, What should be the architecture of an
English people settled in a country lying in the
latitude, though not always in the climate, of Italy ?
Should it be the Gothic of England or the Roman-
esque of Italy ? There seemed much to be said on
either side ; my own mind was finally fixed by the
teaching of experience, by seeing which style
really flourished best on American soil. I found
the modern churches, of various denominations, certainly better, as works of architecture, than I had
expected. They may quite stand beside the average
of modern churches in England, setting aside a
few of the very best. All persuasions have a great
love of spires, and, if the details are not always
what one could wish, the general effect of the
spires is often very stately, and they help largely
towards the general appearance of the cities in a
distant view. But I thought the churches, whose
style is most commonly Gothic of one kind or
another, decidedly less successful than some of the
civil buildings. In some of these, I hardly know
how far by choice, how far by happy accident, a
style has been hit upon which seemed to me far

more at home than any of the reproductions of
Gothic. Much of the street architecture of several
cities has very successfully caught the leading idea
of the true Italian style, the style of Pisa and
Lucca, the style of the simple round arch and
column, uncorrupted by the vagaries either of the
Italian sham Gothic or of the so-called *Renaissance.*
In a large part of the Broadway of New York the
main lines of this style—I speak only of the main
lines, without committing myself either to details
or to material—are very happily reproduced. The
general effect of many parts of that long street
struck me as just what the main street of a great
commercial city ought to be. And there are some
buildings of the same kind in Chestnut Street,
Philadelphia, though there they alternate with
other buildings of a very strange kind, whose
odd fancies make us turn back to look with real
satisfaction on the honest brick of Independence
Hall. Some of the banks especially seem to have
thought that the stumpier they made their columns
the safer would be their deposits. But it was the
capitol at Albany which fully convinced me that
the true style for America was the style of Pisa and
Lucca. The building has a most successful outline ; in its details it is a strange mixture of styles,
not so much confounded together as used side by

side. This is accounted for by the history of the
building, and by the employment of more than one
architect. But the visitor is concerned only with
the result. There are parts which I cannot at all
admire; but there are other parts, those in which
the column and round arch are employed, which
certainly pleased me as much as any modern building that I have seen for a long time. When I
say that the arches of the senate-chamber seemed
to me, as far as their general conception goes,
worthy to stand at Ragusa, some will understand
that I can say no more.

I am almost afraid to add that I thought that
some parts of the City Hall at New York, or more
strictly of the adjoining court-house, were entitled
to some measure of the same praise. For I found
it hardly safe to speak of that range of buildings.
Its name at once drew forth bursts of indignation
at the millions of dollars which certain persons had
contrived to gain for themselves out of its making.
Politically I felt abashed, as if I had somehow
become a champion of corruption. Still I could
not help thinking that the columns and arches, of
which alone I was speaking, were as guiltless of
any offence as Sir Thomas More's beard. So, to
come back to the capitol at Albany, I ventured to
make the very smallest kind of artistic criticism on

some chandeliers in the corridors which seemed to
me too big, as hiding some of the architectural
features. My remark did not call forth any artistic defence of the chandeliers; but I was much
struck at the remark which it did call forth. Some
one or other, I was answered, must have had some
corrupt object in making them too big. It is certainly odd that one cannot make the most purely
artistic criticism, either for or against anything,
without calling up thoughts which have very little to do with artistic matters. Certainly I should
be sorry to think that the architectural forms of
which I speak carry with them any necessary taint
of political corruption. For in these round-arched
buildings I see a good hope for a really national
American style. The thing seems to have come
of itself; and the prospect is all the more hopeful
if it has. I should be better pleased to think that
the forms which pleased me when my eyes were
fresh from Ragusa and Spalato were the work of
men who had no thought of Ragusa or Spalato before their eyes.

This constant talk about local corruption, of
which one certainly hears more at New York than
anywhere else, put a very revolutionary thought
into my head. If New York City really is all that

many of its own inhabitants tell us that it is, would it not be a good thing to carry out a divorce between New York City and New York State? A glance at the map will show how very little geographical connexion there is between the two. In several of the Eastern States, the greatest town stands, owing to the circumstances of the original settlement, in a corner of the State, cut off from its main body; it has therefore been found to be unfit to be the centre and capital of the State. All this is pre-eminently true of New York. With its appendage of Long Island, it lies geographically apart from the body of the State; Buffalo and Rochester seem to stand almost in another world. Yet New York is the greatest city, not only of the State, but of the Union; its population is far larger than that of many, perhaps most, of the States. For such a city not to be in any sense a capital, not to be the head of anything, seems unnatural; it might conceivably be dangerous. Why should not such a city become a separate State of itself? The separation would seem a gain from every point of view. The great island city seems to have nothing whatever in common with the great inland region which bears its name. So great a city seems marked out in every way for a separate being, almost more than any free

city, past or present, of the old world. And if it
be so politically corrupt as it sometimes calls itself, so thoroughly given over to the rule of bosses,
the inland region would surely be all the better for
parting company. *Baselland* and *Baselstadt* are
parted; let the same thing be done on a greater
scale with New York-*land* and New York-*stadt*.
But there would be no need to bring down either
to the rank of a "half-canton." Each would be
a State; each would rank among the greatest
States; each would have its two senators and as
many representatives as its amount of population
would give it. New York would thus stand out
as the greatest of free cities, while one may venture
to think that things at Albany would be a good
deal improved. And, if such a division were carried out, should not Long Island go to Connecticut,
to which it seems to belong geographically, and
which has ancient claims upon it?

XV.

I will wind up with a word or two as to the
American newspapers. In one sense there is
nothing more truly characteristic of the country.
That is to say, the American newspaper is something which stands by itself and has nothing in

Europe at all like it. In another sense there is
no country where the newspapers are less characteristic. That is to say, there is no country which
it would be more unfair to judge of by its newspapers. The American newspaper represents a
level of American life lower than the level of
English life which is represented by the English
newspaper. By newspapers I mean more parti-
cularly the higher class of daily papers, as distinguished both from daily papers of a lower
class, and from weekly papers, which approach
more to the nature of reviews. Several of these
last come, both in appearance and matter, very
much nearer to English papers of the same class
than any daily American paper does to the best
English daily papers. The "Nation" of New York,
for instance, would take a high place in periodical
literature anywhere. There are of course inferior
weekly papers in America, just as there are in England; my point is that there is no daily paper in
America at all on a level with the best American
weekly papers. Of the American daily papers one
may fairly say that the very best do not come so
near to representing the thoughts and feelings of
the best class of Americans as the best English
newspapers come to representing the thoughts and
feelings of the best class of Englishmen. The gap,

I am afraid, is rather wide in either case; but it is certainly much wider in the American case. Even the foremost English papers make not a few displays of silliness and ignorance; it would sometimes not be hard to charge them with the graver faults of lack of principle and consistency. But in one sense they keep up a very high standard indeed; we hardly know how high that standard is till we compare them with newspapers elsewhere. The higher class of English papers are most honourably free from vulgar personality. When I say personality, I do not mean merely speaking evil of people; I mean all mere personal gossip of every kind. "Tremendous personages" indeed, Kings, Presidents, and Prime Ministers, must pay the penalty of their greatness in being more talked about than other men. Perhaps the fashion of talking about them has of late grown somewhat more than is to be wished; but we certainly never see in a decent English paper the kind of gossip even about Mr. Gladstone which we see in otherwise respectable American papers about the obscurest people. Still less does an English daily paper waste its space in discussing or jesting at the personal peculiarities and personal affairs of small folk. I am speaking, as I said, of daily papers. The "society paper" is a new and very unpleasant invention, or rather revival;

I say "revival;" for it is due even to the "society papers" to say that those who are old enough can remember a still worse style of "society paper." But in England the papers openly devoted to personal gossip form a class apart. The great political papers have no fellowship with them. The distinctive thing in the American press is that the foremost daily papers play the part of a society paper, and a very inferior society paper, as well. I suppose that, taking one thing with another, the "New York Tribune" is the best of the American daily papers. It would stand high anywhere both for ability and for character. But even the "New York Tribune" admits personal paragraphs which would certainly never find their way into the "Times," the "Daily News," or the "Standard." The "New York Herald" is a paper which the European traveller cannot help reading, because it is the only American paper which does give some systematic account, though often a meagre and confused account, of general European affairs. It is very big; as a collection of American news, it is wonderful; it is in its own way a marvel of successful enterprise. But its literary level is low, and its "personal" paragraphs are a by-word. It is not that they are always scurrilous; it is their extreme silliness that strikes more than anything else. It is hard to conceive for what kind of people they can be written; certainly not for the kind of people with whom I spent my time in America. The American paper in short is clearly written for a class of readers inferior to the average reader of the English paper.

One or two reasons may perhaps be seen for this difference. Here too I feel sure that the lack of a real capital has something to do with it. A London daily paper, published in the acknowledged capital of the kingdom, aspires to be national. It may chatter about "metropolitan" and "provincial," as though every inch of Great Britain, unless perhaps the county of Middlesex, was not a sharer in the same rights as every other inch. But it would not find it at all pleasant to do without the "provincials" altogether. It will naturally, and often quite rightly, give special prominence to things that go on in London. But the last thing that it would wish is to be a mere local London paper. It means to be read and understood all over the country, and, as far as may be, all over the world. To this end it puts on a national character, and wisely and honourably eschews mere personal gossip. The national character of the great London papers is shown by the fact that a local London press exists by the side of them, for the benefit of those to whom London is really a dwelling-place, and not merely a place for sojourns and meetings. But no American paper can have this national character, because no American city is a national centre in the sense in which London is. As I hinted already, London is New York, Washington, and the capital of each man's own State, rolled into one. The New York papers come nearer than any other to the character of national papers; but they are local New York papers as well. And, for the same reason also, the standard of local papers is higher in England than in America. The daily papers, often written with very high ability, which now appear in our chief towns, are in every way a gain. They are a wholesome influence in times when many things tend to give too great importance to a single centre. They often take a far more thoughtful and less conventional view of things than the London papers. Still it is the London papers whose standard they follow. They must dwell on local affairs and local persons in a way in which a London paper does not. But the London paper has given them the example of keeping themselves, as a rule, from mere gossip, whether scurrilous or simply silly. Even the inferior local papers in England do not indulge in it to the same extent as the American papers. Except when there is something specially exciting, the smaller English local paper is commonly too much afraid of its own public to go in for anything like the "personal" column of the "New York Herald." If there is anywhere in England anything like this last amazing collection of scraps, it must be found in papers which do not make their way into cultivated society. The point to notice is that in America this kind of thing is found in papers which cultivated society can hardly do without.

Another cause is surely to be found in a quarter whither we have traced quite another result, that to which I referred when speaking of certain peculiarities of American pronunciation. The far wider spread of a certain amount of education, of education, one may say, without cultivation, has the same effect on the press which it has on political life. It is not the highest type that sets the standard; it is not even anything which imitates or affects to follow the highest type. The highest type is there, just as much as it is here; but it in a manner keeps itself back; at any rate the daily press does not by preference adapt itself to its tastes. The way in which things are constantly told and discussed, the mere physical look of most of the papers, the sensational air given to everything, the startling headings, the lines of small capitals breaking in upon the ordinary text, all show that the American daily paper is not meant, at least it is not mainly meant, for the higher elements in American society. The refined and cultivated class have to put up with it; but it is another class for whom it is directly meant. The English paper, on the other hand, at least affects to adapt itself to the higher order of tastes. Its efforts are sometimes a little amusing, but that is the object aimed at. Anything glaringly inconsistent with that object is avoided. The American daily paper does not even make the attempt.

I spoke just now of weekly papers in America. There are of course there, as here, weekly papers of various kinds. And the weekly paper anywhere will hardly aim at exactly the same level as the daily paper. Its aim will be either higher or lower. It will try to adapt itself either to better or to worse tastes than the daily paper. I speak of course of weekly papers which are strictly newspapers, which record or discuss the events of the day, not weekly periodicals which are purely literary or scientific. That the higher class of weekly papers should aim higher than the daily paper is almost in the nature of things. The weekly paper of the higher kind is necessarily addressed to a smaller class of readers than the daily paper, and its writers have a longer time to think over what they write. It almost necessarily follows that, either in America or in England, the best weekly papers will be, from one point of view, better than the best daily papers. The point to be noticed in comparing the two countries is that the gap between the best daily and the best weekly paper is much wider in America than it is in England. We see this in matter, in style, in the mere physical look. An American daily paper is often almost as hard to read as a German or a Greek paper, and it further has the sensational headings which the German and the Greek spare us. The American weekly paper has not exactly the same look as the British weekly paper, just as an American book has not exactly the same look as a British book. But the American and the British weekly paper, the American and the British book, are simply varieties of the same thing. The American and the British daily paper must be set down as two essentially different things.

I do not think that in what I say of American papers I am speaking from any personal feeling. Among my American experiences I must certainly reckon my personal experiences of the American press; but those experiences have been of a very varied kind, and they have certainly awakened in me much more of amusement than of any other feeling. I have had the honour of having a good many things said of me in American papers, some friendly, some unfriendly, some neutral. Nor am I in any way amazed at sayings either friendly or unfriendly. What did sometimes amaze me was that sometimes a paper which was friendly one day would be unfriendly the next, without my being conscious of having done anything meanwhile that could account for the change. My friends in such cases sometimes resorted to the usual way of explaining anything unpleasant. An Irish contributor must have crept in unawares. And I might also say that some of the things that were said of me were perfectly true, some utterly false, while some had that mixed character, that gathering of imaginary details round a certain kernel of fact, which I conceive to be the true notion of a myth. It felt odd at first to have one's looks and one's clothes described and criticized in print; but one gets used to it as to other things. And if some disapproved of my trowsers and some of my "accent," it made up for it to find oneself described as "a man of might, used to move whole continents." I had certainly not rated my own powers of mind or body at anything like that measure; but a vanity which I trust was harmless could not but be pleased at finding that there were those who thought me capable of such great deeds. One ought not to review one's reviewers; but I drew forth one or two bits of criticism so choice that I cannot bring myself to let them go. For instance, I was seized on by a Roman Catholic paper, very Irish indeed, for a sportive suggestion made earlier in these pages when parts of them appeared in their periodical shape. I had hinted, in the gaiety of my heart, that the United States would be the better if certain Irishmen were hanged, and I added that many people in America thought so too. I had always fancied that it was another people, and not the Irish, who needed a surgical operation to get a joke into them. But it is a fact that I was gravely charged and solemnly condemned for the crime of instigating to wholesale murder. I did feel it a little hard that my Irish critic was so fierce at a mere suggestion of hanging, while he passed by without a word, what he must have seen in the very same page, a plainer saying on behalf of Home Rule than most Englishmen would have dared to write. I shall be tempted to believe that Home Rule is of less value than I thought it, if no Irishman is to be found who is ready even to be hanged for its sake.

One or two censures of a less serious kind
have also caused me some amusement. That
I "have yet much to learn in American history"
is a lighter charge than that of stirring up a
whole continent to a general massacre, and it is
moreover a charge to which I must unreservedly
plead guilty. But a New York paper once went
about to prove the fact in an odd way. I said in
one of my lectures that "several Presidents have
held office for two consecutive terms." I was
simply discussing the question whether re-election
of the President was desirable or not, a question
which I had discussed in full eighteen years before
in my essay on Presidential Government. The
exact number of Presidents who had been re-
elected, as it was of no importance to the argument, was certainly better away. But I was taken
to task for imperfect knowledge of American
history, because I said "several Presidents" and
did not give the exact number "six." Now, if I
were in a cavilling fit, I might answer that the
Presidents of whom I spoke have a perfect right
to say "we are seven." The list runs: Washington, Jefferson, Madison, Monroe, Jackson, Lincoln,
Grant. For, though Lincoln did not live through
his second term, yet he was elected to it, which is
all that concerned my argument. My ignorance

was further proved by my saying that " in the earlier times of the Union the President addressed Congress in a speech, like a King's speech: in later times he has sent only a written message." This matter too I had spoken of nineteen years before;* and the names of the Presidents were of no importance to my argument. But my critic wondered what I could mean by " later times," when the President who made the change was one who lived so long ago as Jefferson. Possibly my critic's standard of "later times" may differ from that of one who was for a while contemporary with Jefferson; but I could not help taking refuge this time in the Irish theory. For surely no native-born American citizen could have thought, as the critic seemed to think, that the presidency of Jefferson was not a later time than the presidencies of Washington and the first Adams.

But there is one feature of the American news-paper system which the New World surely has all to itself. At all events, it is in the Old World brought to bear only on those exalted persons who must be prepared for everything. One is used to have odd things, though perhaps not quite such

* History of Federal Government, i. 291.

odd things as one sees in America, said of one in
the newspapers of one's own land. But the interviewer, the man who asks you questions simply in
order to print your answers in a newspaper, is, as
far as my experience goes, purely American. To
be sure I was interviewed before I left England,
and that by a fellow-Britisher; but then he was in
the employ of a New York paper, and his portrait of me appeared at New York as soon as I
landed. After I reached America I was interviewed a good many times. The process is not
always pleasant; for the questioning largely consists in asking for one's impressions on various
American matters, and specially on points of likeness and unlikeness between America and England.
It is certainly odd that, when so many American
papers are always assuring the world that they do
not care for British opinion, they should still be
so untiringly anxious to find out what British
opinion is. And the questioning on these points
sometimes puts one in an unfair dilemma. If one
blames anything, one runs an obvious chance of
giving offence. And if one praises anything, one
runs the chance of giving offence on the subtler
ground of being thought "condescending" and
"patronizing." Another subject on which the
interviewers were very anxious to get something

out of me was Ireland. On that subject I had my own reasons for keeping strict silence. I was also asked a good many questions about myself, and I seemed to arouse a good deal of amazement whenever I had to explain that I was not a professor and that I did not live in a town. I fancy too that I sank a good deal in the opinions of some of my questioners when I had to tell them that I knew nothing about Mr. Oscar Wilde, whose name was then to be seen in large letters on the walls, as his photographs, in various attitudes, were to be seen in the windows, at Washington and at several other places. It was too true that I had never heard of Mr. Wilde till I took up his poems in the house of a gentleman in Massachusetts. I afterwards learned more about him from a lady at Washington, who showed me a poem of Mr. Wilde's which won the Newdigate prize at Oxford. The subject was Ravenna, and in it one half-line was given to Theodoric. But I was sometimes pressed on much more amazing subjects. An interviewer at Cincinnati seemed to think himself wronged because I could tell him nothing whatever in answer to what seemed to me a very strange question; "Do you think there is most drunkenness on Sunday afternoons in English or American cities?" An interviewer further west represented me as saying that, the further west I went, the *better* I found the newspapers. I had not ventured on any such invidious comparisons. I had kept myself to what I thought the safe and undeniable remark that the Western papers were *bigger* than the Eastern. On the whole, I got used to the interviewers, and I was specially charmed with the moral portrait of me which was given by one of them at St. Louis. From him I learned that, when I don't know a thing, I say that I don't know it, and that, when I do know a thing, I speak as if I were quite certain about it. To the interviewer, as I gathered from his report, this way of acting seemed a little strange, though he clearly approved of the eccentricity. To my own mind the puzzle would be why any man should either pretend to know a thing that he does not know or pretend not to know a thing that he does know.

But it must not be thought that the process of interviewing is a privilege or a punishment set apart for the stranger. It is equally the lot of the native. As far as I could see, not only must every public man expect to be interviewed whenever it is thought to be for the public good, but every private man must expect to be interviewed whenever it is thought that the world in general has a right to know about his private affairs. I remember one very strange case. I do not bear in mind the exact details; but the main part of the story was that a certain father had refused his consent to his daughter's marriage with a certain suitor. There were some odd features in the story, and the father's refusal led to a very pretty quarrel, rising, I think, to something like a breach of the peace. In no part of the world could either tongues or pens be expected to keep from wagging on such provocation as this. But it did seem a strong measure when a New York interviewer, catering for the public information, forced himself on the disappointed and wrathful lover, and asked for a minute account of all his actions and feelings during the whole business. For once the interviewer was baulked; the young man altogether refused to make a father confessor either of the interviewer or of the public which he represented. But it was easy to see from the tone in which the interviewer told his tale that he held that the refusal was a deep wrong done both to himself and to every newspaper-reader in the country.

XVI.

I spoke a little while back of two or three bits of criticism on myself in American newspapers, to .

which I could refer with simple amusement. I
will end my story by speaking of another criticism
of a graver character, which however I might not
have spoken of, if it had not opened a line of
thought of some moment with regard to the great
events of the last two-and-twenty years of American history. It is only natural that the great civil
war should still be largely in men's minds, and it is
perhaps not very wonderful that that touchiness of
which I spoke long ago, that readiness to imagine
slights, even to look out for slights, which is so
characteristic of a large class of people in America,
reaches its height on all points connected with the
civil war. To be sure, that war has already become
almost mythical; President Lincoln, though he
died only eighteen years ago, has already become
something more like a deified hero or a canonized
saint than simply a great ruler, with his merits and
his faults like other men. ⁓ In the eyes of a great
many he is one whom it is not enough to admire,
on the whole to approve; you must bow down. Of
course this superstition is not to be found among
the best class of Americans; but it is exactly the
state of mind which is largely represented by the
newspapers. It would seem to be thought patriotic to give out that a man has said something
against the cause, even when nothing of the kind

has been said or thought. I have heard it cruelly said that there are some women who, if they have to take a journey alone, think themselves wronged if they are not insulted by some man before they come to the end of it, and who in such a case invent, or perhaps really imagine, some tale of the kind which has not happened. If this be so, it is an odd form of an odd kind of self-consciousness and self-importance. But experience seems to show that the thing is possible. Certainly a feeling of the same kind seems to find a place in the minds of some American newspaper-writers. To no other source can I trace one comment at least which has been made on myself, and that in a quarter where I did not look for it. At mere absurdities it is easy to laugh ; it is another thing when one finds oneself charged, on a very grave matter, with having done what one never did, and what was one of the last things that one would have wished to do. I was certainly a good deal amazed, I was even tempted to be a little angry, when I read such words as the following. They came in the "Boston Advertiser," October 7, 1882, a paper which up to that time had been very civil to me. The writer was discussing what I said about the use of the names "British" and "English," and his immediate reference was to a remark quoted

by me * from an American friend, which he oddly
mistook for a " suggestion" of my own.

Mr. Freeman is entirely mistaken in suggesting that the use
or the disuse of the word [British] had anything to do with
America's liking or disliking for England. Of that liking or
disliking he professes not to understand the key. Here it is.
In 1810, Mr. Allston wrote, and wrote truly:—

> While the manners, while the arts,
> That mould a nation's soul,
> Still cling around our hearts,
> Between, let ocean roll,
>
> Our joint communion breaking with the sun,
> Yet, still, from either beach
> The voice of blood shall reach,
> More audible than speech, " We are one!"

Up till 1861 whenever that stanza was repeated at a public
meeting in America, the house rang with applause. Till 1861
Americans supposed it was true; in 1861 this nation looked to
"Britain" for sympathy in a great struggle. At the hands of
the governing classes of "Britain" she received nothing but
insults; from the lips of Mr. Freeman, among others, she received scornful ridicule. From the working men of England
she received cordial sympathy. It is to that period only that
there dates back the indifference which Mr. Freeman thinks
he observed, as to the right which Americans have to claim
the English name.

Now an outburst like this fairly takes one
aback. It goes beyond the common licence which

* See p. 29.

one grants to people who write in a hurry. It
distinctly states the thing that is not. I do not
exactly see why I am reckoned among the
" governing classes," seeing that I have never had
so much as a seat in Parliament. But it is more
important to ask when, where, and how, " America"
ever " received scornful ridicule from my lips."
" Lips" ought in strictness to imply speeches, and
I certainly did not make any speeches on American
matters. But will the " Boston Advertiser" be
good enough to give me a reference to any passage
of my published writings, where I have spoken
of the United States, or their constitution, or
anything to do with them, with " scornful ridicule"? Will he show me any passage in which I
speak of them otherwise than with the respect and
interest due to a great English commonwealth, one
whose constitution has been one of my special
objects of study? He will certainly find passages
which will show that, when the United States were
split asunder for a season, I was not a fanatical
partisan of either side. But surely to hold that
there was something to be said on both sides in a
great quarrel, though certainly much more to be
said on one side than on the other, is not the same
thing as throwing " scornful ridicule" on either
side, least of all on the side on which one holds

that there is most to be said. Let me here state exactly what my position was with regard to the American civil war, because I fancy it was a position which was not shared by very many. I never for a moment doubted the formal right of the Northern cause, or, to speak more accurately, the cause of the Federal Government. That right no man could doubt who had given any serious thought to the first principles of a federal constitution. Secession was formally rebellion, just as much as rebellion against a king. Nor could I see that the Southern States had any of those reasons to justify their rebellion which have often fully justified rebellion against kings, and sometimes against commonwealths too. Still I could not help seeing that the rebellion of a sovereign State—in a federal system those words are not contradictory, and in England we have had a rebel king—is something practically different from the rebellion of private men. I could quite understand that many men, who were personally opposed to secession, who may even have voted against secession, might, when their States actually seceded, honestly deem it their duty to go with the State. And, though I fully admitted the formal right of the Federal Government to bring back the seceding States by force, I greatly doubted

the wisdom of exercising that right. Had a
single inland State seceded all by itself, had even
South Carolina remained alone and not been
joined by any others, I could then have had
no doubt as to the wisdom of its exercise.
It seemed different when the seceding States
formed one large section of the country, quite
able to all appearance, from its extent and geographical position, to form a great confederation for themselves. I did doubt whether it was
wise in such a case to try forcibly to bring the
seceding States back into a relation from which
they wished to escape. It seemed too much like
the Frenchman's alternative, "Be my brother, or
I will kill you." That, even granting the rightful-
ness of the war, I could not at the time approve of
every step taken by the Federal Government is, I
trust, not unpardonable. I could not unreservedly
pledge myself to approve of every act even of Mr.
Gladstone. If I had lived in the ninth century, I
might have held myself free to exercise my own
judgement even on the acts of Alfred. If, for a
while, I expected the result of the struggle to be
other than it was, I certainly judged wrongly;
but I assuredly was not alone in wrongly judging.
And fully holding, as I did, the abstract right of
the Federal Government, simply doubting of the

wisdom of exercising that ˙right, acknowledging
that it was for them, not for me, to judge of that
wisdom, it is not very wonderful if, as the war
went on, my sympathies turned more and more to
the Northern side, and if, when the war ended, I
could fully rejoice in its ending. If my Boston
critic, instead of making a random attack, had
taken the trouble to find out what I really said,
he might have been dissatisfied with me as a
somewhat lukewarm supporter, but he would not
have risked a saying so utterly contrary to the
truth as that I ever treated the cause of the Union
with " scornful ridicule."

Now this way of talking springs from a state of
mind which is very easy to understand, because
it arises from causes which are common to all
mankind, and which we may see at work in full
force among ourselves. But it further shows
that state of mind as affected by the peculiar
relations between the mother-country and its
independent colonies. To every citizen of the
United States the Union naturally was and is
very dear. The feeling of its greatness, the pride
in its greatness, is a feeling of essentially the same
kind as the ordinary Briton's pride in the greatness
of the "British empire." But it is the same feeling
in a much higher shape; pride in the greatness

of a brotherly union is surely a nobler feeling than
pride in mere dominion. And I conceive that
this natural and praiseworthy feeling of pride in
the Union was not confined to the citizens of the
Northern States, but was to be found in Southern
bosoms also. It might be overcome by a yet
stronger feeling; but I conceive that no citizen of
the South, though he might bring himself to look
on secession as the only means to compass his ends,
would have sought secession for its own sake so
long as he could hope to maintain the Union on
his own terms. Indeed there is some reason to
think that, in most of the Southern States, secession was not at first the wish of the majority.
It was rather the wish of a zealous and active
minority, which, as always happens in such cases,
overcame a majority which had no wish to destroy
the Union, but which was not willing to give itself
much trouble to maintain it. When secession was
once voted, when war had once begun, men who had
had no wish to secede fought heart and soul against
compulsory union. Their position I hold to have
been formally wrong and the position of those who
fought for the Union to have been formally right;
but the position of both sides is perfectly intelligible. I suspect that most of us, if we had
chanced to be born in the Northern or the

Southern States, would have done as most people in the Northern and the Southern States severally did. But the Englishman of Britain, at least as the case seemed to me, had no call to share in the passions of either side. Wishing well to his brethren in either section of the Union, he would regret that any strife, above all that such a strife, should have arisen between them. But in the feeling for the Union, as an object in itself, a feeling perfectly natural and praiseworthy in the Northern supporters of the Union, he could not be expected to share. The welfare and freedom of his American kinsfolk were a great deal to him, but the Union, a mere means towards securing that welfare and freedom, might well be very little to him. He might naturally say, " Let my brethren of the Western continent form one confederation or two or a dozen, as they may think best; however they may arrange themselves, I shall wish well to all of them." This would be a natural view for an Englishman of Britain who was not pulled by any strong prepossessions of his own towards a more zealous championship of one side or the other. But it is not a state of mind into which either the North or the South could be expected to enter. Both sides looked for something more. The men of the Northern States, loving the Union, deeming the Union unjustly torn asunder, naturally looked for sympathy to the men of the elder land. Looking on themselves as the representatives of the United States, and thereby of the English folk on the soil of the United States, looking on the States that had seceded as members that had by their own act cut themselves off from the common fellowship, it was perfectly natural in the men of the Northern States to expect from their British kinsfolk, not only the general interest and good will of kinsfolk, but a special interest and sympathy in the special work in which they were engaged, the maintenance of the Union. It was not wonderful if they forgot that the maintenance of the Union could not be to their British kinsfolk an object as precious for its own sake as it was to themselves. Nor was it wonderful if they forgot that the men of the Southern States also might, just as naturally from their own point of view, if not just as rightfully, look for sympathy from their British kinsfolk. Now both sides got sympathy in plenty from different classes and parties in Great Britain; it is of course part of the charge against Great Britain that the South got any sympathy at all. My Boston critic complains that what he calls the " governing classes"—among whom I find myself so strangely reckoned—bestowed upon the North "nothing but insults."

This is undoubtedly true of a great many, and it is much to the shame of those of whom it is true. So far as British sympathy for the South arose from dislike or jealousy of the North, no feeling could be more unworthy. Northern indignation at the treatment which the North received from a large class in England is perfectly just ; and even Northern disappointment at finding that England in general was not prepared to take up the Northern cause with all the fervour of the North itself, though not perfectly just, is perfectly natural. Still it is a little unfair, when a Northern writer speaks as if no kind of people in England but "working men" had shown any good will to the Northern cause. This is hard upon not a few English scholars and public men who were as zealous for that cause as any English working man could be, almost as zealous as any born Northerner could be. Among them I do not claim to be reckoned ; as I never was a partisan of the South, I never was an enthusiastic partisan of the North. But it is surely unfair to charge one who did not indeed share the passions of the North, but whose intellectual convictions were on the Northern side, with having treated the North with "scornful ridicule."

It was in truth perhaps impossible for one to whom the subject of Federal Government was a

matter of scientific study to enter strongly into
the passions of either side. While the American
Union was parted asunder and put together again,
I was reading and writing how the Achaian Union
was put together, parted asunder, and put together
again. Had the federal form of government been
cast aside for some other, it might have been a thing
to stir up some indignation. Had the Union been
overthrown by a tyrant, it would indeed have been
a thing to stir up a great deal of indignation. But
when one federal body split into two, the thing
was too curious a study for a scientific observer
of federalism to get very angry either way. He
might even be sometimes tempted to some slight
satisfaction at his range of observation being en-
larged. And one thing at least he might do
which was hardly of the nature of "scornful
ridicule." My Boston critic can hardly know how
often I worked during those years, both in
acknowledged and in anonymous writings, to
answer the fallacies which were endlessly put forward by the English supporters of the South. As
in many other cases, men were led astray by the
misuse of a name. As the government of the
United States was a federal government, the word
"Federal" naturally got into everybody's mouth.
The "Federal Government," the "Federal army,"

&c., did so and so. Many people in England seemed to think that the word "Federal" was, not a general name for governments of a particular class, but the particular name of the Government of the United States. I firmly believe that some of them would have been surprised if any one had chanced to speak just then of the Federal Government of Switzerland. The one side were "the Federals;" the other side were "the Confederates." Many seemed quite to forget that the two names, though for the nonce applied to two hostile sets of people, in themselves meant exactly the same thing. Because they disliked one particular federal government, they turned their dislike into an argument against the federal principle in general, forgetting that all the while they were backing up one federal government against another. That certain members of a federal union had chosen to separate from it was held to prove the inherent worthlessness of all federal union. They who so argued did not stop to think that this argument told just as much against the Southern Confederation as against the original Union; they did not stop to think that the same argument would equally tell against kingly government. If certain parts of America had shown themselves dissatisfied with federal rule, many more parts of Europe had shown themselves dissatisfied with kingly rule. During the years when I was supposed to have employed myself in loading "America" with "scornful ridicule," I was really rather largely employed, not exactly in supporting the cause of the North, but in answering fallacies of advocates of the South which hindered any fair discussion of the points really at issue between the two parties. I will venture to reproduce a specimen of the kind of language which I really used, and to which the name of "scornful ridicule" is surely somewhat strangely applied.

It is the American system, in its most essential features, which forms the natural object for the imitation of other communities of Englishmen beyond the seas. It is for them to seize on the leading principles of the immortal work of Washington and Hamilton, to alter such of its general provisions as experience has shown to be defective, to work in such changes in detail as may be needed by any particular commonwealth. The American Constitution, with its manifest defects, still remains one of the most abiding monuments of human wisdom, and it has received a tribute to its general excellence such as no other political system was ever honoured with. The States which have seceded from its government, the States which look with the bitterest hatred on its actual administrators, have re-enacted it for themselves in all its essential provisions. Nothing but the inveterate blindness of party-spirit can hinder this simple fact from at once stopping the mouths of cavillers. Sneers at republics, at democracies, at federal systems, are, wherever they are found, mere proofs of ignorance and shallowness; but there are no mouths in which they are so utterly inconsistent, so utterly self-condemning, as in the mouths of champions of the Southern Confederation.*

There are doubtless some to whom it will be matter of offence that I have, even in the above passage, implied that the great men of the American Union were after all only men, and that their work shares the common imperfection of human things. With such I cannot argue, and I do not think that any rational person in the United States will expect me to argue. But the state of mind which is displayed by this feeling is really a very curious subject of study. Some people in America seem really to think that the United States, their constitution and all that belongs to them, did not come into being by the ordinary working of human causes, but sprang to life by some special creation or revelation. They think themselves wronged if it is implied that they are not absolute *autochthones*, but that they are the kinsfolk of certain other nations. They think themselves wronged if it is implied that their institutions did not spring at once from the ground, but that they were, like the institutions of other nations, gradually wrought out of a store common to them with some other branches of mankind. That the people of the United States have a right

---

* Historical Essays, First Series. p. 406.

to a great inheritance of past ages, that the whole
history of civilized man is a possession in which
they have a lawful share, is in the eyes of these
reasoners a reproach from which they are eager to
escape. Those who teach such a doctrine deny
them " all originality." It is certainly an odd taste
when a man who has a perfect right to an unbroken
and illustrious pedigree would rather be taken for a
chance child picked up by the road side ; but such
seems really to be very like the frame of mind of
some on the other side of Ocean who are anxious to
maintain the " originality" of all American things.
One might be curious to know whether they think
that the English language and the Christian religion
were invented on American soil after 1776. The
wish to be " original," in the sense that is meant,
the wish to have no history, no traditions, no connexion with the past in any shape, is surely the
oddest wish ever framed. Happily for the American branch of our people, they have as little claim
to " originality" in this sense as the British
branch. The founders of their commonwealth
were men too wise to seek after " originality" of
that kind. The best witness to that truth is the
comparison with another set of reformers who did
strive to be " original." The year 1789 opened
somewhat different æras in America and in France.

The conservative wisdom of the founders of the American constitution gave their people the old institutions of their own folk, modified as change of place and circumstance called for. Their work, not being " original," has lived on ; it has gone through the most frightful of trials ; but it abides and promises long to abide. The " original" work of the men who strove to break with the past in all things has another tale to tell. Revolutions, restorations, tyrannies, new schemes warranted to last for ever and breaking down at the first trial of their strength —such is the outcome of "originality" in political institutions, a fruit of which happily neither branch of the English folk has tasted.

To come back for a moment to myself, I believe that my own great fault, a fault which I see in some quarters is deemed unpardonable, is that I have more than once used the words "disruption of the United States." In all that I have thus far said in this section I have spoken wholly of what has been said in newspapers ; but, while I was at Baltimore, I was met by a visitor from a distant State, Wisconsin I think, who told me, with perfect civility but with a good deal of emphasis, that, when he saw those words in the title-page of a volume of mine, he would not look at any page that came after. And I can see by various references in newspapers that the use of the word is thought to be something about which I may fairly be twitted, something which shows how utterly I failed to understand what was going on twenty years back. And I confess that, in the early stages of the struggle, I did in one way fail to understand; that is, I expected that the struggle would have another issue from that which it had. But that has nothing to do with the word " Disruption," which is a simple statement of an undoubted fact. I do not like the word; that is, I would rather use an English word, if I could think of one; but it must be an English word of exactly the same meaning. That there was a disruption of the United States, that is, that part of the United States split away from the rest, that for a while there were two federal bodies where there had before been only one, is among the plainest facts of history. That the divided body was again united in no way gets rid of the fact that it once was divided. I more than once answered objectors with a parable. " If you should be so unlucky as to break your leg, and a skilful surgeon should set it so well that you could walk just as well as you could before, still that happy cure would not get rid of the fact that your leg had been broken." In short, if there were no disruption, how came there to be any civil war at all? The civil war

came of secession, and the secession of some of the
members of the body is the disruption of the whole
body. What happened to the American Union in
the nineteenth century A.D. had happened to the
Achaian Union in the third century B.C. In both
cases there was disruption; in both cases there was
reunion. This unwillingness to look a simple historical fact in the face, and to call it by its natural
name, is surely the very height of national touchiness. I can hardly conceive such a feeling in any
other case. A Venetian would hardly make it a
point of national honour to put out of sight the fact
that there was such a thing as the League of Cam-
bray, and that that league was followed by a disruption of the Venetian dominions far more thorough than happened either in the Achaian or in the
American case. He would rather dwell on the endurance and energy of his commonwealth, on the
strong heart which was able to bear up through
such a fearful trial, and to win back again the provinces which had been lopped away.

It is surely high time for this abiding soreness
on a point of past history to pass away. There
has been disruption; but it has been followed by
reconstruction. The one process implies the
other; without disruption, there could have been
no need for reconstruction. It is best to say as

little as possible about the disputes of twenty
years back. The discussion has no longer any
practical use, and it is plain that the time has not
yet come for discussing such points in a purely
historical spirit. .I should myself have been
inclined to say nothing about them, had I not,
long after I took my pen in hand, found myself
made the subject of a charge as amazing as
it is untrue. It is a pity to tear open wounds
which are fast healing. As far as I could make
out, the South is getting reconciled to its lot
quite as speedily as could be looked for. It is
admitted that the restoration of slavery is as
little to be wished for as it is to be hoped for.
The women and the clergy are understood to be
less ready to accept the new order of things than
the male laity; but it is to be supposed that they
too will come round in course of time. Things
are taming down; the negro, though no longer a
slave, is falling back into his natural place. The
Congress of the Union contains Senators and
Representatives who once fought against the
Union. The former Vice-President of the Confederate States held, while I was in America, a
prominent place among them. It is surely high
time, not to forget the past, which cannot be, but
to put out of sight its needless visible memorials.

It is unpleasant to see, in this and that collection, specially in the capitol at Albany, some kinds of trophies exhibited which would hardly be in perfect taste, even if they had been won from a foreign enemy. If

Bella geri placuit nullos habitura triumphos,

there are some spoils of victory which might as well be kept out of sight. I confess that it gave me a turn to see, among honest memorials of the War of Independence, among memorials of other kinds of the great men of the Union, little personal relics of fallen soldiers of the South. The miniature of a lady taken from the body of a slain Confederate officer is hardly as yet an object for the public gaze.

I have spoken somewhat freely; but it is only towards printed matter that I have had any need to use freedom. My personal reception everywhere was as kind and friendly as any reception could be. And I believe that I am right in judging of the rational class of the American people by that reception, far more than by their newspapers. Not that I would have it thought for a moment that I have any serious ground to complain of the American press as a whole. Some strange things have been

said of me, and one very false and unpleasant thing;
but I have had many pleasant things said of me also
and amusing things without end. I have no wish
to dwell on any personal matter save so far as to
make my answer to one very hateful charge; but,
in giving my impressions of the United States, I
could not well help saying how I had been im-
pressed, both in a general and in a personal way,
by a thing which fills so important a place in the
United States as its newspaper press.

And, once more to fall back on my old doctrine
of the common heritage of the two severed
branches of the English folk, let me end by saying
that they have something like a common mythology.
Some of those stories which go about the world
with blanks for the names have shown themselves
both in England and in America, and have had the
blanks filled up with different names in the two
countries. I used to hear a story in England, which
in England was quartered at Manchester. There
was during the great war with France a clergyman
of the collegiate church who was a zealot in loyalty.
A child was brought to him to be christened, and
the parents or sponsors wished to give the babe the
startling name of " Napoleon Boneyparty" (I spell
the last word as I have not the slightest doubt

that it was sounded; the Tuscan surname kept its four syllables for a long time within my memory). "None of your Jacobin names here," cries the patriotic priest; "George, I baptize thee." I go to New England; I there hear how a child was brought to be christened by a minister who was at least equally zealous on what, by a kind of analogy, may be called the same side of the question. "Name this child;" "Thomas Jefferson." The clergyman, yet fiercer than his Manchester brother, cries out, "I can't give him the name of the devil; John Adams, I baptize thee." The story is so good that it would be a pity if either side of the Ocean should set up any exclusive claim to it. Let both waive all pretensions to "originality," and let the tale abide as a common possession of the English folk.

To clothe the same thought once more in a graver shape, what I have done in this present attempt has been to put on record some of my chief impressions on the most striking points which come home to a traveller in the great English land beyond the Ocean. I naturally look at things from my own point of view; let others look at them and speak of them from theirs. To me the past history and present condition of the United States is, before all things, a part of the general history of the Teutonic

race, and specially of its English branch. Of that
history the destiny of the American commonwealths,
as far as it has already been worked out, forms no
unimportant part. And their future destiny is undoubtedly the greatest problem in the long story of
our race. The union on American soil of so much
that is new and so much that is old, above all the
unwitting preservation in the new land of so much
that is really of the hoariest antiquity in the older
world—the transfer of an old people with old institutions to an altogether new world, and that practically a boundless world—supply subjects for specu-
lation deeper perhaps than any earlier stage of the
history of our race could have supplied. Like all
other human institutions, the political and social
condition of the United States has its fair and its
dark side; the Union, like all other human communities, must look for its trials, its ups and downs,
in the course of its historic life. It has indeed had
its full share of them already. The other members of
the great family may well be proud that the newest,
and in extent the vastest, among the independent
settlements of their race, has borne, as it has borne,
a strain as hard as any community of men was ever
called on to go through. And we of the mother-
land may watch with special interest the fortunes of
that branch of our own people on whom so great a

calling has been laid. Truly we may rejoice that, with so much to draw them in other ways, that great people still remains in all essential points an English people, more English very often than they themselves know, more English, it may be, sometimes than the kinsfolk whom they left behind in their older home.

THE END.

INDEX.

INDEX.

Books, difficulty of obtaining, in America, 187; German, mass of, 187.

Bosses, the rule of, 129, 130, 131; meaning of name, 158; importance of Irish, 158.

British, opinion, importance of, in America, 6, 7; opinion, sensitiveness to, in America, 7; opinion, odd ways of showing yearning for, 8, 9; possible reason and date of substitution of name "English" for, 27, 28, 270; hardly expected to be conversant with some American matters, 43, 44; Museum MSS., 186, 187; point of view in civil war, 274 to 279.

Briton, use of word, 29.

Car, railroad, 60, 61.

Carriages, railroad, 60, 61; hackney, high fares, 229, 230.

Centre, intellectual and social, in America, 218; comparison between France and America in this respect, 219; of England, London, 214, 216, 218, 256; no national, in America, 256; Washington not a, 217; New York not a, 216, 217.

Centralization, tendency to, 111; danger of, 111, 112.

Chester, city of, 243.

Chicago, city of, 245.

Chinese, under consideration of Federal Legislature, 153; bills, 153; distinction between Indians, negroes, and, 154; comparison between Jews in Russia and Chinese in America, 154; control of European newspaper press, possible effect, 155; anti-, riots in America, 155; ques-

Chinese—(Continued).
tion outside of America, 155.

Churches, Roman Catholic, 160; lack of antiquity in, 161; indiscriminate use of word, 162; ideas suggested by interior of, 164; Baptist, in Brooklyn, 164, 165; arrangement of, 165, 166, 167; at Newport, 165, 166; talking in, 167; in Virginia, 171; Episcopal the fashionable, 173, 174; State, 176, 177; architecture, 160, 246.

City, likeness of English and American, 11; history of word, 64; distinction between town and, 64, 65; power of mayor in, 122, 123; election of mayor of English, 129; election in Philadelphia, 129, 130, 131, 132; no central, in America, 215; contrast of small town with great, 220; of Chester, 243; position of American cities, 244, 245; law and government of, in America, 91 to 107; politics and government of, in America, 107 to 159.

Citizenship, indiscriminate bestowal of, impossible, 158; mean standard of, possible, 159.

Civil War, touchiness concerning, 268; author's position in regard to, 272; Northern expectations during, 277, 278, 279; time for calm discussion of, not come, 287; trophies of, 288.

Clergymen, use of word, 162; position of, 175, 176.

Colleges, number of, 179, 180; power of granting degrees, 180; advantage of inferior, 181; Federal power in

Great Britain, theoretical chance of coloured Lord Chancellor in, 156; barbarian subjects of, 156, 157.

Greek, analogy between use of word "English" and, 25, 26; history parallel with New England, 197, 198.

Guiteau, trial of, 94; criticism of judge in trial of, 96, 97; indictment of, 97; argument of insanity of, 98.

Harvard, College, 180; men of learning at, 188; competes with Yale, 188, 189; dominant theology at, 191; commencement at, 196;

Heredity, introduction of principle of, impossible in United States, 136, 137.

History, tendency of Americans to forget their early, 44; teaching of, in schools, defective, 45; of three Englands, 48; historical nomenclature, 71, 72; value of original authorities in, 184, 185, 186, 187, 188; local American, study of, 196, 197, 199, 200; parallels in, 197, 198; study of, at Johns Hopkins University, 199, 200; American, author charged with ignorance of, 262.

Hotel, American, 237, 238; clerks, 237, 238; status of guests in, 238; tendency to live in, 239.

Independence, war of, feeling arising from, 21, 22; war of, influence in snapping ties, 22, 23; war of, names used, 27, 28; war of, churches previous to, 161.

Indians, called "dark Americans," 151; school at Car-

Indians—(Continued).
lisle, 151; possible elevation of, 151; preferred to negro, 151; pride of whites in descent from, 152; personal appearance of, 152; at Schenectady, 152, 153; distinction between Chinese, negroes and, 154.

Intonation, English, 42, 85, 86.

Inventions, modern, political advantage of, 235, 236.

Ireland—Irish, comparisons between England, America, and, 12 to 14; vote, 139, 142; Home Rule, 140; element mischievous in English lands, 140; element bad in American politics, 141; English misrule in, 142; assimilation of, 142, 143; question, importance of, to English folk, 158; "bosses," 158; intrusion, signs of, in churches, 160; ascendancy, streets of New York a protest against, 228; bondage in hack fare, 231.

Jurisprudence—Justice, centralization of, 92; conservatism of American, 94; essential principles of English, found in States, 94; administration of, in rural districts, 98, 99; in Virginia, 99; of peace, 99, 100, 101.

Language, in America, 50 to 91; community of, 49, 50; follows law of colonies, 52, 53; of railroads, 60, 61; abuse and corruption of, 67, 68; slang in, 67, 68; printer and schoolmaster foes to, 87, 88; no real difference of, 91.